THE USBORNE
CHILDREN'S
ENCYCLOPEDIA

THE USBORNE

CHILDREN'S ENCYCLOPEDIA

Jane Elliott and Colin King

With the help of Susan Crawford and Annabel Craig

Research by Ingrid Cranfield
Designed by Sylvia Tate
Edited by Angela Wilkes

Contents

What is the Earth?

The Earth is a huge ball of rock spinning in space. It is not a perfect ball as it is slightly flattened at the top and bottom. The equator is an imaginary line around the widest part. The top half of the Earth is called the northern hemisphere and the bottom half is called the southern hemisphere.

Earth Facts

The Earth measures about 40,000km around the equator. It would take a month to drive around it at 55km per hour.

The Earth weighs about 6,000 million million million tonnes.

The highest temperature ever recorded was 57.7°C in the Sahara Desert, in Africa. This is hot enough to fry an egg on the sand.

The lowest temperature ever recorded was minus 88.3°C in Antarctica. Antarctica is the coldest and windiest place in the world.

About one fifth of the land is desert. Deserts are the hottest and driest places on Earth. They have less than 250mm rain per year.

Near the equator it is hot all the year round and it rains nearly every day. The land around the equator is called the tropics.

Thick, green forests called rainforests grow in the tropics. Tropical rainforests contain over half of all the types of plants and animals in the world.

Only about a quarter of the Earth's surface is land. There are seven big pieces of land, called continents. Most of the land is in the northern hemisphere.

Nearly three quarters of the Earth's surface is covered by sea. The four oceans are all joined together. You could sail right round the Earth without seeing land.

Many mountains are too high and cold for plants and animals to survive there. Mount Everest, the highest mountain on Earth, is 8,850 metres high.

About a tenth of the Earth's surface is always covered with ice. The further you travel from the equator, the colder it is. The Poles are the coldest places on Earth.

Air and the atmosphere

The Earth is surrounded by a layer of air about 500 kilometres thick, called the atmosphere. It stops dangerous rays from the Sun burning up life on Earth.

We cannot see air but we feel it as wind. It is made up of many gases, such as oxygen, which we breathe, and carbon dioxide, which is used by plants.

The higher you go into the atmosphere, the less air there is and the harder it is to breathe. That is why people carry oxygen tanks when they climb mountains.

All our weather happens in the first twelve kilometres of the atmosphere. Above this, there are no clouds and the Sun always shines in the daytime. Aircraft usually fly higher than the weather, about 13-22 kilometres above the Earth.

The Earth in Space

The Solar System

The Earth is one of nine planets that circle the Sun. They are kept in orbit by the pull of the Sun's gravity*.

Together they make up the Solar System. It was probably formed from dust and gases billions of years ago.

Mars is sometimes called the "red planet" because it is made of red rocks.

Earth is probably the only planet which has water.

Mercury is the planet closest to the Sun. It is a little bigger than our Moon.

Venus is so bright, it is often mistaken for a UFO – an unidentified flying object. Its surface is hidden by thick, white clouds.

Jupiter is mostly gas with a tiny rocky core. It has sixteen moons.

What does the Sun do?

The Sun gives the Earth light and warmth. Without it, the Earth would be in constant darkness and too icy cold for anything to survive.

The Sun is so far away that it takes eight minutes for its rays to reach Earth. It is so big that you could fit over a million Earths into it.

How hot is the Sun?

The Sun is a gigantic ball of burning gases. Its surface temperature is 5500°C. A pinhead as hot as this could kill you from 150km away.

*You can read more about gravity on page 120.

The asteroids are thousands of rocks which go around the Sun between Mars and Jupiter.

Planet data

Use this chart to work out the order of the planets from biggest to smallest. Which one takes the longest to orbit the Sun? Which one is the furthest away from the Sun?

Name of Planet	Diameter	Distance from the Sun	Time taken to orbit the Sun
	kilometres	kilometres	years
Pluto	2,300*	5,950 million	248 years
Neptune	49,530	4,497 million	165 years
Uranus	51,120	2,870 million	84 years
Saturn	120,540	1,427 million	29.5 years
Jupiter	142,800	778 million	12 years
Mars	6,790	228 million	687 days
Earth	12,600	150 million	1 year = 365 days
Venus	12,100	108 million	225 days
Mercury	4,880	58 million	88 days

Neptune sometimes travels beyond Pluto and becomes the furthest planet from the Sun.

Uranus is circled by rings of dust.

Saturn is made of mainly gas and has rings of dust and ice circling around it. It has eighteen moons.

Pluto was first sighted in 1930. Scientists now consider it to be a dwarf planet.

Sunspots and solar flares

Sunspots are dark areas of gas which are slightly cooler than the rest of the Sun's surface. Solar flares are giant jets of gas that shoot up millions of miles.

WARNING Never look directly at the Sun as its brightness could damage your eyes.

Watching an eclipse

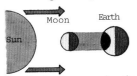

Sun   Moon   Earth

A total eclipse happens when the Moon passes exactly in front of the Sun and blocks off its light for a few minutes. You can see a total eclipse of the Sun from any place on Earth, but you might have to wait for about 400 years.

*Approximate measurement

A moon is a ball of rock that circles a planet. Most of the planets in our solar system have moons. You can see them on pages 8-9.

Our Moon has no light of its own and is lit up by light from the Sun.

Who is the man in the Moon?

It looks as if the Moon has a face because rocks on the surface make dark shadows.

Eclipse of the Moon

An eclipse of the Moon happens when a full Moon moves into the shadow behind the Earth.

During the eclipse, the Sun's light cannot reach the Moon so it looks as if it has vanished.

The dark side of the Moon

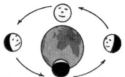

We never see one side of the Moon because the same side is always facing the Earth.

The Moon's far side was a mystery until photographed by a space probe in 1959.

Why does the Moon change shape?

The Sun lights up different parts of the Moon as it orbits the Earth. This makes the moon look as if it is changing shape.

It takes the Moon 27.3 days to circle the Earth. The different shapes of the Moon are called phases.

There is a new Moon when the Moon is between the Sun and the Earth and we see only a sliver of the lit-up part.

Each night for the next two weeks we see more and more of the lit-up surface as the Moon orbits the Earth.

There is a full Moon when the Moon has travelled halfway around the Earth and we can see all the lit-up surface in the sky.

Over the next two weeks, the Moon appears to shrink as we see less and less of the lit-up surface.

Stars

A star is born

A star begins as a ball of gas that shrinks and becomes hot. The gas burns, which makes the star shine. It may shine for 10,000 million years.

As the gas is used up, the star explodes or shrinks. The tiny star, called a white dwarf, is almost dead.

Measuring the Milky Way

Our Solar System is somewhere here

Our Sun is a star in a galaxy (star family) called the Milky Way. The Milky Way has 100,000 million stars. Scientists believe there may be 6,000 other galaxies scattered through space.

The huge distances in space are measured in light years. A light year is 9.5 million million km. A spacecraft travelling at the speed of light would take millions of years to reach Earth.

How do we know?

Astronomers are scientists who study the stars. Until recently, they only had their eyes or simple telescopes to rely upon.

Now, more powerful telescopes on satellites can "see" deep into space and send information back to Earth. Space probes are sent to explore the planets.

Manned space shuttles take off like rockets and land like gliders. They carry all sorts of useful scientific equipment into Outer Space.

Comets and meteors

Comets sometimes appear as they orbit the Sun. They are balls of dirty ice and have long tails.

A shooting star is a meteor or rock burning as it enters the Earth's atmosphere.

How the land moves

How old is the Earth?

The Earth was formed about 4,600 million years ago. At first, it was a fiery mixture of boiling rock and poisonous gases.

As millions of years went by, the Earth grew cooler and a thin crust of solid rock formed on its surface.

What is inside the Earth?

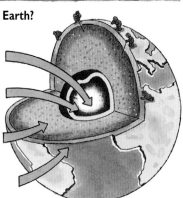

It is 6,300km to the centre of the Earth. The temperature there is as hot as the Sun.

The very middle of the Earth is called the core. It is a solid ball of melted iron.

The mantle is a layer of soft, flowing rock. Towards the surface, it is hot and liquid.

The Earth's crust is made of hard rock which is split into sections called plates.

What happened to the supercontinent?

Scientists think the continents may once have been joined as a giant piece of land called Panagaea.

About 190 million years ago movements in the Earth's crust made it break up. The pieces of land are still moving.

How mountains are made

Mountains take millions of years to form. Sometimes the Earth's crust is squeezed up to form fold mountains.

Block mountains form when the Earth's crust splits and one side is slowly pushed up.

When melted rock below the Earth's crust slowly forces land upwards, dome mountains are formed.

Earthquakes and volcanoes

When the ground trembles and shakes, it is called an earthquake. Earthquakes can split and crack the ground, destroy buildings and cause floods and fires.

A volcano is a place where red-hot liquid rock, called lava, forces its way up a crack from deep inside the Earth. The lava hardens as it cools, to form a mountain.

Geysers and mudsprings are found near volcanoes. Steam and boiling mud are signs of the Earth's heat escaping.

Many active volcanoes are under the sea. Scientists try to predict when the sleeping (dormant) ones will erupt again.

Earthquakes and volcanoes often happen close together where the plates that form the Earth's crust join.

A fault line is where two plates of the Earth's crust rub against each other deep down and make the ground move.

Eruptions

The volcano Paricutin suddenly erupted in Mexico in 1943. In two years, it had grown 457 metres high and 16 kilometres wide. Every day, it blew out 100,000 tonnes of lava.

Tidal waves

After lying dormant for over 200 years, a volcano called Krakatoa, in Indonesia, exploded in 1883. The explosion caused a tidal wave 41 metres high which killed over 36,000 people.

Under the ground

Burrowing down

The Earth's crust has several layers. The top layer is soil, which is made of crushed rock and the remains of plants.

Small animals, plants and insects burrow into the soil and help break it up.

Below the soil there is a small layer of stones.

Underneath everything there is a layer of solid rock.

How are rocks made?

Rocks are formed from the minerals that are found in the Earth's crust. Different rocks contain different minerals and they are grouped into three families depending on how they are formed.

Igneous rock
Hot, molten rock bubbled up from deep inside the Earth, then cooled and hardened into rocks such as granite and basalt.

Sedimentary rock
Rock that has built up in layers over millions of years. It is made from tiny bits of rock, sand or shells which have been washed into the sea or a lake.

Metamorphic rock
Mainly sedimentary rocks that have changed in some way by being squeezed or heated deep inside the Earth.

These bits of rock sink to the bottom and over millions of years they harden together into solid rock.

Earthquakes sometimes force sedimentary rock up from the sea-bed so it becomes part of the land.

Minerals

Some minerals do not form rocks. They grow into mineral crystals under the ground. Each mineral has different shaped crystals.

Everyday minerals

Minerals are used to make all these everyday objects.

Precious minerals

Gemstones are very beautiful and rare. They are used to make jewellery.

Wearing down the land

Rain, wind, frost and ice all slowly break rocks down into smaller pieces. This wearing down of the Earth's surface is called weathering and erosion.

Old, weather-beaten mountains are usually lower and more rounded than recently formed ones.

Caves are formed by water wearing away rock under the ground.

The weather often wears rocks into strange shapes.

Useful things from the ground

We dig mines and drill wells to take coal, oil, metals, salt and many other useful things from the ground.

Oil and natural gas have been formed over millions of years from the fossils of tiny sea creatures which were preserved in rock.

Coal is the remnants of ancient swamp plants that were preserved in rock and hardened over millions of years.

Metal minerals, such as gold and silver, have to be separated from rock before they can be used.

Finding fossils

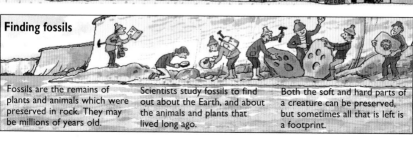

Fossils are the remains of plants and animals which were preserved in rock. They may be millions of years old.

Scientists study fossils to find out about the Earth, and about the animals and plants that lived long ago.

Both the soft and hard parts of a creature can be preserved, but sometimes all that is left is a footprint.

Time

Why do we have day and night?

The Sun's light gives the Earth its day and night. The Earth spins like a top in Space at 1,690km per hour at the equator. It takes 24 hours to spin around once.

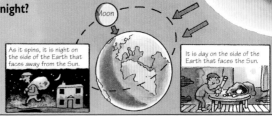

As it spins, it is night on the side of the Earth that faces away from the Sun.

It is day on the side of the Earth that faces the Sun.

Where do the stars go?

During the day, the stars are still in the sky but we cannot see them because the Sun's light is much brighter than they are.

Why does the Sun set?

The Sun does not move at all, but as the Earth spins around, it looks as if the Sun rises in the east and sets in the west.

Me and my shadow

Light always shines in straight lines, so you can see shadows behind anything in its way.

At midday the Sun is directly overhead and the shadows are very short.

Early in the morning and evening the Sun is low in the sky, so the shadows are long.

Morning

Midday

Evening

Ways of measuring time

Long ago, hunters kept track of the days by counting how many times they went to sleep at night.

Knights used sand timers to time their tournaments. The tournament ended when all the sand had run through.

People used sundials. During the day the Sun's shadow is cast onto the dial and moves around to mark the time.

Going clockwise

The Ancient Egyptians divided day and night into hours. They measured a stick's shadow against an hour scale.

At night, they filled a pot with water. As the water ran out through a hole, they read the hour marks on the side.

It was hard for people to meet when they all measured time differently. They needed a standard measure of time.

In 1581, Galileo, an Italian scientist, saw that the swing of a lamp always took the same length of time, no matter how big it was.

This led to the invention of the pendulum clock. A pendulum clock keeps time with a swinging weight called a pendulum.

Now, very accurate atomic clocks can measure time by the vibrations of atoms, the tiny particles of which everything is made.

Keeping up with the times

Every minute of the day somewhere around the world there is a sunrise, a sunset, a midday or a midnight.

When flying west, you put your watch back an hour for each time zone that you cross. When flying east, you put your watch forward an hour.

The world is divided into 24 time zones. On a map, lines of longitude show the zones. The gaps between the lines show how far the Earth spins in one hour.

If you cross the International Dateline, you change your calendar, not your watch. You lose a day going west and gain a day when you go east.

Why do the seasons change?

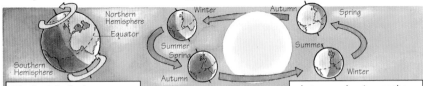

The Earth is tilted to one side, so as it spins around the Sun, different hemispheres are nearer to the Sun.

It is summer in the hemisphere that is tilted towards the Sun and winter in the other one.

Autumn and spring are the in-between seasons when the two hemispheres are the same distance from the Sun.

Sandman or snowman?

The two hemispheres have opposite seasons from each other. When it is summer in one, it is winter in the other.

Long days and short days

Summer days are longer than winter ones because the hemisphere that is tilted towards the Sun stays in the Sun's light for longer.

The land of the midnight sun

Because of the Earth's tilt, the North and South Pole are always far from the Sun. It is always cold and icy there.

It is dark for nearly 24 hours a day in the winter. In the summer, the Sun shines all night as well as all day.

About 300 years ago, some British criminals begged to be hanged rather than sent to spend the winter in the dark.

It never rains but it pours

Lands on the equator are always hot because this part of the Earth is never tilted away from the Sun.

Places close to the equator do not have a summer and winter. They just have a dry season and a rainy season.

In the rainy season, winds blow in from the sea, bringing moisture. They blow the other way in the dry season.

Seasonal changes

Winter

Winter is the coldest season. The days are short and it gets dark very early. There is snow and frost in many countries.

Plants stop growing and most trees have no leaves. Some animals grow thick coats to help them keep warm.

Other animals hibernate and sleep all winter. People wear warm clothes and spend most of their time indoors.

Spring

In the spring, the days grow longer and warmer. Buds appear on the trees and plants begin to grow again.

Birds return from the warmer countries where they have spent the winter. They build their nests and lay their eggs.

Animals look for mates and have their babies. People do more things outside again in the warmer weather.

Summer

Summer is the warmest time of year. The days are long and it does not get dark until late. Everything grows well.

Flowers bloom, fruit ripens on the trees and crops ripen in the fields. There is plenty for birds and animals to eat.

People spend more time outside enjoying the sunshine. Many of them go on holiday to places such as the seaside.

Autumn

In the autumn, the days begin to get shorter and colder. Plants stop flowering and leaves fall from the trees.

There is plenty of fruit, berries and nuts on the trees and bushes, and the crops in the fields are harvested.

Animals and farmers store away food for the winter months, and some birds fly away to warmer countries.

19

Weather

What is weather?

Our daily weather is caused by a mixture of three things: sun, air and water. The Sun gives us warmth, the air moves to make the wind and water makes the clouds, rain and snow.

The same rain over again

The water that falls as rain was once water in the sea, rivers, lakes and even puddles. It has fallen millions of times before.

The Sun

Every day, the Sun heats up the water and some of it becomes tiny, invisible drops of moisture in the air.

Clouds

As the warm air rises, it cools down. The tiny drops of moisture turn into millions of larger drops of water that we see as clouds.

Cloud clues

Cumulus clouds mean fine weather. They are white and fluffy. Large, dark clouds usually bring bad weather.

Stratus is usually a layer of thin, pale grey cloud covering the whole sky. It is often a sign of light rain or drizzle.

Nimbus are grey rain clouds with ragged edges. If they have white, cauliflower-shaped tops, they may bring storms.

Hurricanes and tornadoes

A hurricane is a violent storm that can destroy buildings. Hurricanes usually happen in tropical areas.

A tornado, or whirlwind, is smaller, but faster and just as dangerous. It will suck up or destroy anything in its path.

If a tornado happens over the sea, it sucks up gallons of water forming a giant waterspout.

Hailstones are frozen raindrops. They blow about in the clouds and build up layers of ice around them.

Fog and mist are clouds close to the ground.

Rain

As the air becomes colder, more drops of water form. They become too heavy for the cloud and fall to the ground as rain.

Cirrus are wispy and streaky. They are a sign of wind. They float very high up and are made of ice crystals.

Snow

If it is very cold, the water drops freeze to form ice crystals. Then they fall from the clouds as snow.

Why the wind blows

When air is warm, it rises and cold air flows in beneath it. When air moves around like this, it makes wind.

Thunder and lightning

When the weather is bad, electricity builds up inside the clouds. Lightning is a giant spark of electricity escaping.

The lightning heats the air around it. The hot air pushes against the cooler air and makes the sound of thunder.

Rain and melted snow drain into rivers and the sea. Then the water begins its journey all over again.

Some winds blow right across the world as hot air from the equator rises. Cold air from the Poles takes its place.

Rainbows*

A rainbow appears when the Sun shines through raindrops. The colours are always in the same order: red, orange, yellow, green, blue, indigo and violet.

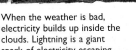

*You can find out more about rainbows on page 106.   21

Climate

Why are there hot and cold places?

When people talk about climate, they mean the type of weather that a place usually has in each season.

How hot or cold a place is depends, among other things, on how far it is from the equator*, where it is always hot.

Land far from sea is often dry, as sea winds do not carry their moisture that far. In the middle of a continent, the summers are hot and the winters cold.

Land near the sea has cooler summers and warmer winters than inland. Warm or cold ocean currents flowing near the coast may also affect the climate.

It usually rains a lot near mountains and the higher you go, the colder it becomes. Even near the equator, mountains have snow all the year.

Steamy rainforests

Thick rainforests (or jungles) grow in the tropics near the equator, where it is very hot and rains heavily every day.

Plants and trees grow fast and very close together there. Plants can grow to the size of trees and the trees are amongst the tallest in the world.

The forests teem with plants and creatures that live nowhere else in the world. Many could die out because rainforests are being cut down and destroyed.

Few people live in rainforests as they are too hot and sticky. Tribes have to live on plants they find, and hunt whichever animals they can.

22   *You can find out more about the equator on page 6.

Life in the deserts

Most deserts are in the tropics. They are the hottest and driest places on Earth and very few plants and animals can survive there.

Camels can survive for days without water. They live on food or fat stored in their humps.

There are two types of desert – rocky deserts and sandy deserts. In sandy deserts, the wind blows the sand into hills called dunes.

It rains very rarely and when it does there are usually violent thunderstorms and floods. One desert in Peru had no rain for 400 years.

An oasis is a waterhole where people take their animals to drink. Farmers grow crops and date trees and there may be a town.

The Poles

The North and South Poles are the coldest places on Earth. It is very cold because the Sun never shines directly on these parts of the Earth. There is frozen land at the South Pole, but at the North Pole, there is just a slab of thick ice, called the icecap, floating on the ocean.

Icebergs often break away from the sheets of ice and float away until they melt. More than three-quarters of an iceberg is hidden below water.

Arctic people live near the North Pole. The only land animals at the South Pole are visiting scientists, but penguins, whales and seals live in the seas.

If the ice at the Poles melted, the level of the sea would rise by over 70 metres. This would submerge New York, London and Paris completely.

Rivers and lakes

Rowing down the river

A river begins as a spring flowing out of a hillside, or as a stream from a lake.

As the stream flows downhill, rainwater and other streams flow into it.

At the beginning of its journey the young river flows through narrow valleys with steep sides.

The river carries rocks and sand with it and these grind away the banks on each side.

As the river grows larger, it wears away more land and the valley becomes wider.

Most rivers wind their way downhill to the sea, usually along the easiest course.

At the sea

The place where the river flows into the sea is called the river mouth.

Some rivers fork out near the sea. This type of river mouth is called a delta.

A river mouth where the coastal tides flow in and out twice a day is called an estuary.

Lakes

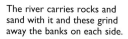

A lake is a hollow filled with water. Sometimes it is water that was left behind when a river changed its course.

Lake Baikal in Central Siberia is the deepest lake in the world. It is 1,940 metres deep at its deepest part.

New Zealanders used to swim in the crater lake of an active volcano. The volcano kept the water hot.

Floods

Rivers can flood and cause damage. The Hwang Ho River in China, changed its course by 480km when it flooded.

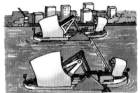

A flood barrier across the Thames River, in England, stops very high tides from flooding London.

Some rivers are blocked by dams, which make hydro-electric power. The valley behind the dam becomes a lake.

Frozen rivers

A glacier is a river of ice that moves very slowly down a mountain. In the summer, it melts back a little.

Most glaciers only move a few centimetres a day, but the Quarayaq Glacier, in Greenland, moves 20-24 metres a day.

In the Ice Ages, glaciers moved across much of the land, carving out deep U-shaped valleys and mountains.

Waterfalls and daredevils

Water wears away soft rock faster than hard rock, making a step in the riverbed. The water falls over the step as a waterfall.

In 1859, Charles Blondin, a French acrobat, crossed the Niagara Falls on a tightrope 48.8 metres above the water.

In 1929, Al Faussett, an American, sailed over the Shoshone Falls in his canoe. The falls are 70 metres high.

River records

The longest river in the world is the River Nile in Africa. It is over 6698km long and flows into the Mediterranean Sea.

The Amazon River is the biggest river in the world. Over 15,000 smaller rivers flow into it on its way to the sea.

The highest waterfall is the Angel Falls in Venezuela. It is 979 metres tall, higher than a 220 storey building.

The Seas
Warm and cold water

The seas cover three-quarters of the Earth's surface. There are warm seas near the equator and frozen seas in the Arctic and around Antarctica.

Currents are rivers that flow in the sea. They drift from hot to cool regions around the world. Currents are also caused by the winds and by the way the Earth spins.

Why is the sea salty?

Rivers wash salty minerals from the rocks into the sea. Some salts are used by animals to build their shells.

The saltiest seas are small, inland seas. The Dead Sea, in Jordan and Israel, is so salty nothing can live in it.

If all the sea dried up, the salt would make a wall around the equator 282km high and 1.5km thick.

What are waves?

Waves are ripples made by the wind. The water seems to move forward but really moves up and down like the sailors' rope.

Waves can travel hundreds of kilometres. They only grow tall and topple over, or "break", when the sea becomes shallow.

Tsunamis are enormous waves up to 50m high, caused by earthquakes under the sea, or volcanoes on the sea-bed.

Tides

On most seashores, the height of the water rises and falls twice a day. These changes are called high and low tides. They are caused by the pull of the Moon and Sun.

The Moon has a pulling effect on the seas. As the Earth spins around each day, the seas on the side nearest to the Moon rise higher, making a high tide.

Underwater lands

If all the water was drained from the sea, the sea-bed would look like the land with plains, valleys and mountains.

Lighthouses warn sailors of underwater rocks that could wreck their boats.

Coral reefs are walls made from the hard shells of small jelly-like animals called corals. They are found in shallow tropical waters.

An island is really the tip of an underwater mountain sticking up out of the sea.

The highest mountain in the world is the underwater mountain, Mauna Kea, in Hawaii. It is over 10km high.

The depths of the oceans have hardly been explored at all. They are pitch dark, as no sunlight reaches them.

At Challenger Deep in the Pacific Ocean, you would have to wait over an hour for your line to sink 11.5km to the ocean floor.

Better late than never

A message was thrown overboard from a ship off Australia and found 72 years later on a nearby island.

After his ship *Benlomond* sank, Poon Lim, a Chinese seaman, survived on a raft for 133 days before he was rescued.

In 1982, a Tudor fighting ship, the *Mary Rose*, was salvaged from 12 metres of mud, 400 years after sinking.

Explorers

Old ideas about the Earth

The Ancient Egyptians thought the land was a god lying down with trees and plants sprouting from his body.

They believed that the sky was a huge goddess leaning over the Earth and the stars were the jewels in her robe.

Ancient Greeks thought the Earth was a flat disc floating on water. The sky was a dome held by a god called Atlas.

Long ago, people believed the Earth was flat and that sailors might sail over the edge into the mouths of monsters.

Some sailors believed that to cross the world, they had to sail through a "fire zone" where the sea boiled.

Now we know that we live on a round ball spinning in space and the force of gravity stops us from falling off.

Why not stay at home?

Many explorers have risked their lives to find new lands for farming or trade, or just for the adventure.

Over 700 years ago, Marco Polo, from Venice in Italy, went overland to China.

In 1492, Christopher Columbus wanted to find a new sea route to India. He sailed off course and landed in America instead.

In 1519, Hernando Cortes, a Spanish explorer, fought the Aztecs in Mexico for their gold and land.

Over a hundred years ago, David Livingstone spent many years in Africa, searching for the source of the River Nile.

Captain Scott raced Roald Amundsen to the South Pole. Scott lost the race and died on his way back.

Finding the way

Long ago, before there were any maps, explorers used the Sun and the stars to help them find their way.

The Pole Star showed them north and south, and they knew east and west from where the Sun rose and set.

They also watched for other clues, such as birds flying towards land, and winds and sea currents.

Sailors measured the height of the Sun or stars above the horizon to find out where they were.

Then they worked out their latitude (how far north or south they were) or longitude (how far east or west).

Later, explorers used a compass to find their way. A compass has a needle that always points north.

Finding the way back

The first maps were drawn by explorers to help them find their way home and show people where they had been.

The maps showed the shape of the land, distances between places and special features such as caves and old trees.

Nowadays, maps show the towns and villages, and the roads, railways, rivers and mountains.

Symbols are used to show all the different things on a map and there is a key to explain what the symbols stand for.

Over the centuries people explored most of the Earth and put together the map of the world we use today.

People still go on exploring but these days the only unknown places left are the depths of the oceans and Outer Space.

Africa

There are seven continents on the Earth. Africa is a huge continent made up of 49 countries and over a billion people live there. Between them, they speak about a thousand different languages. In the north, there is a vast desert, called the Sahara Desert. There are also thick rainforests where it rains every day, and dry plains where giraffes, zebras and lions live.

African Countries

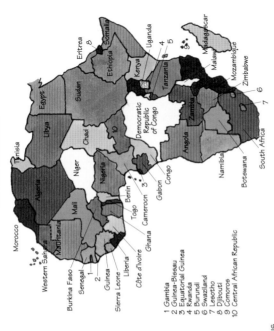

1 Gambia
2 Guinea-Bissau
3 Equatorial Guinea
4 Rwanda
5 Burundi
6 Swaziland
7 Lesotho
8 Djibouti
9 Comoros
10 Central African Republic

Where Africa is in the world

Indian Ocean

Madagascar

MOZAMBIQUE

Mount Kilimanjaro

crop spraying

Mount Kenya

BEIRA

NAIROBI

Masai

coffee growing

Addis Ababa

Ethiopian Highlands

Blue Nile

Lake Victoria

KAMPALA

Lake Nyasa

KHARTOUM

White Nile

Mount Ruwenzori

Lake Tanganyika

River Zambezi

Temple of Zimbabwe

River Limpopo

DURBAN

JOHANNESBURG

HARARE

BULAWAYO

LUSAKA

pygmies

cotton picking

River Congo

Victoria Falls

bushmen

gold mining

Drakensberg Mountains

Mount Cameroon

oil drilling

Lake Chad

River Niger

LAGOS

LUANDA

Kalahari Desert

River Orange

Table Mountain

CAPE TOWN

Atlantic Ocean

ACCRA

Côte d'Ivoire

TIMBUKTU

harvesting cocoa nuts

31

The Americas

The Americas run from the cold lands near the North Pole to Antarctica. The largest jungles on Earth are around the River Amazon in Brazil. Most of the people in North America are descended from European immigrants. They mainly speak English. Most South Americans speak Spanish, except in Brazil, where the people speak Portuguese.

Where the Americas are in the world

Arctic Ocean

Bering Sea

Atlantic Ocean

Caribbean Sea

Pacific Ocean

icebreaker ship

fur traders

plane dropping water to put out forest fire

Yukon River

Giant Redwood Trees

SAN FRANCISCO

LOS ANGELES

VANCOUVER

EDMONTON

SALT LAKE CITY

Rocky Mountains

ice hockey

cowboys herding cattle

DENVER

Rio Colorado

GUADALAJARA

Sugar and Mexico cacti

Rio Grande

WINNIPEG

ST. LOUIS

oil wells

HOUSTON

NEW ORLEANS

MEXICO CITY

Marlin boat

Inuit people fishing

iron and gold mined in this area

QUEBEC CITY

BOSTON

NEW YORK

WASHINGTON DC

Lake Superior

Lake Huron

Michigan

Cotton fields

MIAMI

Appalachian Mountains

Mississippi River

space rocket taking off from Cape Canaveral

transatlantic liners

32

American countries

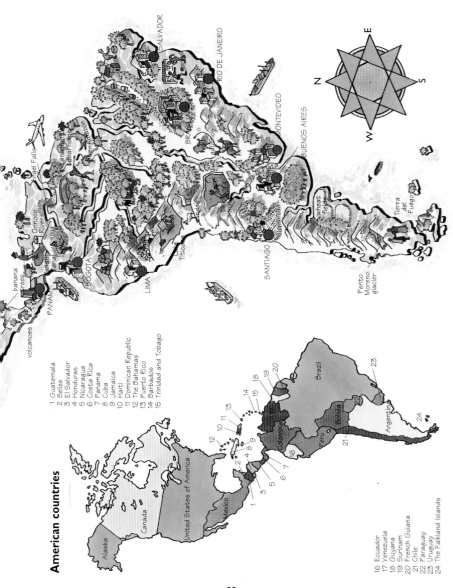

1 Guatemala
2 Belize
3 El Salvador
4 Honduras
5 Nicaragua
6 Costa Rica
7 Panama
8 Cuba
9 Jamaica
10 Haiti
11 Dominican Republic
12 The Bahamas
13 Puerto Rico
14 Barbados
15 Trinidad and Tobago

16 Ecuador
17 Venezuela
18 Guyana
19 Surinam
20 French Guiana
21 Chile
22 Paraguay
23 Uruguay
24 The Falkland Islands

volcanoes
banana trees
Orinoco River
Angel Falls
PANAMA
BOGOTA
Machu Picchu
San Martin
Amazon
LIMA
Titicaca
Andes
SANTIAGO
Perito Moreno glacier
Tierra del Fuego
wheat fields
BUENOS AIRES
MONTEVIDEO
Pampas
BRASÍLIA
RIO DE JANEIRO
SALVADOR

N
E
S
W

Asia

Asia is the largest continent in the world, and makes up nearly one third of the Earth's land. The highest mountain in the world, Mount Everest, is in the Himalayas in Asia. Some countries are very cold and dry while others are hot and wet. Over half the people in the world live in Asia. China alone has over 1200 million people, more than any other country in the world.

Where Asia is in the world

Asian countries

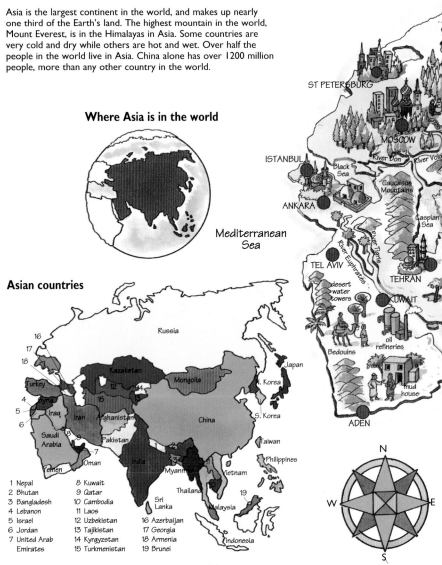

1 Nepal
2 Bhutan
3 Bangladesh
4 Lebanon
5 Israel
6 Jordan
7 United Arab
  Emirates

8 Kuwait
9 Qatar
10 Cambodia
11 Laos
12 Uzbekistan
13 Tajikistan
14 Kyrgyzstan
15 Turkmenistan

16 Azerbaijan
17 Georgia
18 Armenia
19 Brunei

Arctic Ocean

woolly mammoth found in ice here

Bering Sea

large fish factory ship

NIZHNIY NOVGOROD

Ural Mountains

Trans - Siberian railway

ULAN-BATOR

VLADIVOSTOK

Mount Fuji

Cossack Horseman

Yurt

camel cart

Hall of Prayer

KYOTO

TOKYO

OSAKA

harvesting wheat

Gobi Desert

BEIJING

River Hwang Ho

weaving

KABUL

Great Wall of China

planting rice

SHANGHAI

Pacific Ocean

Potola Palace, Lhasa

Himalayas

Chang Jiang Yangtze River

River Indus

Mount Everest

DELHI

River Ganges

HONG KONG

Minarets of Hyderabad

Taj Mahal

River Irrawaddy

HANOI

MANILA

MUMBAI

HYDERABAD

RANGOON

Buddhist Temple, Rangoon

Mekong River

MADRAS

BANGKOK

HO CHI MINH

Malaysian village

long house

COLOMBO

SINGAPORE

Indian Ocean

JAKARTA

35

Australia and New Zealand

Australia is the largest island in the world, and the smallest continent. New Zealand is nearly 2,000km from Australia. Until about 300 years ago, the only people living in these countries were the Aborigines in Australia and the Maoris in New Zealand. Since then, however, many Europeans have settled there.

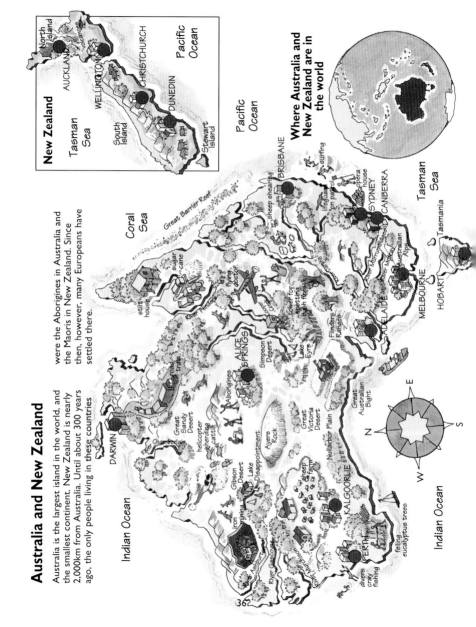

Where Australia and New Zealand are in the world

Antarctica

Antarctica is almost as large as the United States of America and Australia put together. No plants or animals live there apart from a few penguins and seals near the sea. Several nations have sent expeditions to claim sections of the land.

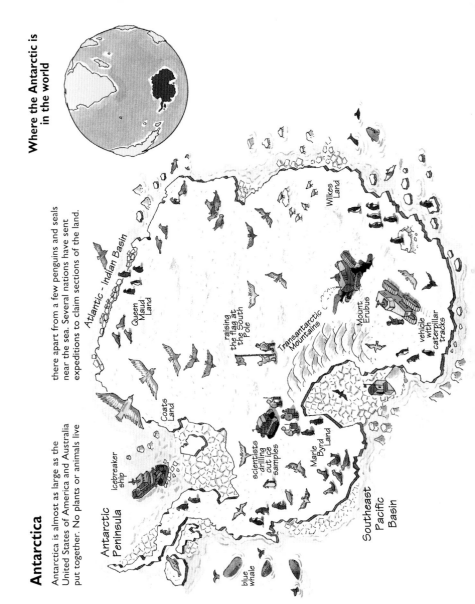

Where the Antarctic is in the world

Antarctic Peninsula

icebreaker ship

blue whale

Coats Land

Queen Maud Land

Atlantic - Indian Basin

raising the flag at the South Pole

scientists drilling out ice samples

Marie Byrd Land

Southeast Pacific Basin

Transantarctic Mountains

Mount Erebus

vehicle with caterpillar tracks

Wilkes Land

Europe

Europe reaches from Ireland in the west, to the beginning of Asia in the east. Many different languages are spoken throughout Europe. It has a mild climate, so much of the land is good for growing things, and it has reserves of oil, coal and iron ore.

Where Europe is in the world

European countries

1 Albania
2 Andorra
3 Belgium
4 Liechtenstein
5 Luxembourg
6 Monaco
7 Netherlands
8 San Marino
9 Switzerland
10 Czech Republic
11 Slovakia
12 Hungary
13 Slovenia
14 Croatia
15 Bosnia-Herzogovina
16 Yugoslavia
17 Macedonia
18 Lithuania

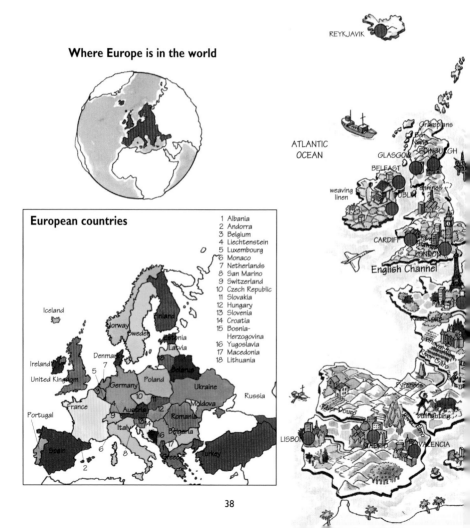

REYKJAVIK

ATLANTIC OCEAN

Grampians
Ben Nevis
GLASGOW
EDINBURGH
BELFAST
weaving linen
DUBLIN

CARDIFF
LONDON

English Channel

River Douro
Pyrenees
River Garo
Loire

LISBON
MADRID
VALENCIA

Iceland
Norway
Sweden
Finland
Denmark
Estonia
Latvia
Ireland
United Kingdom
Poland
Belarus
France
Germany
Ukraine
Austria
Moldova
Russia
Portugal
Italy
Romania
Bulgaria
Spain
Greece
Turkey

The Earth's story

The Earth was formed about 4,600 million years ago from gas and dust. It was so hot that it became a ball of liquid rock. As time went by, its surface cooled and formed a hard crust.

Scientists think that over millions of years the shape of the land and the climate changed. Some animals died out and others appeared which could survive in the new conditions.

Where the seas came from

3,800 million years ago

The hot Earth was covered with thick clouds of steam and gas. As the temperature cooled, it began to rain. It rained for hundreds of years and the seas formed.

For the first thousand million years, there was no life on Earth. During this stormy time, mountains were formed and worn away. The land was covered by the sea and then left dry again.

Where life began

3,500-500 million years ago

The first living things on Earth were too tiny to be seen and lived in the seas.

Later, sea plants formed. They gave out oxygen, which the first sea animals needed to breathe.

Fish were the first animals with a backbone and a kind of skeleton inside their bodies.

Life in the swamps

500-280 million years ago

As more land appeared out of the seas, living things spread onto the wet land. Many plants grew there and animals could now feed on land.

Over a long period of time some types of fish developed lungs. They could breathe out of water and drag themselves along with their strong fins.

These animals, amphibians, could live both on land and in water. Along with many insects they lived in the warm, steamy swamps covering the Earth.

Reptiles

280 million years ago

The climate on Earth grew hotter and the swamps dried up. Amphibians needed water to lay eggs, so many died out. Animals, called reptiles, developed. They laid eggs on the land and were able to live in the new conditions.

Monster reptiles, the dinosaurs, roamed the Earth. Some of them were 30 times bigger than an elephant. Many of them ate plants. Some reptiles, called pterosaurs could fly. Dinosaurs died out about 60 million years ago.

Mammals

190 million years ago

Scientists do not know exactly why the dinosaurs died out, but 150 million years before they did, the first mammals appeared on Earth.

Mammals feed their babies on milk that the mothers produce. It was about now that the first flowering plants grew.

Man and the million year winter

From 2 million years ago

The climate grew cold and the Ice Ages began. Only mammals with fur, such as mammoths which lived in the last Ice Age, could survive on the land.

About 150,000 years ago, in the last Ice Age, an early type of human being lived in caves. They made stone tools and knew how to light fires.

Scientists think that in 5,000 million years' time the Earth will end. By then the Sun may have grown to 100 times its size and could burn up our planet.

41

Plants and flowers

There are over 350,000 different types of plant in the world. All living things depend on plants for their survival.

Plant power

People and animals need the oxygen which plants give off so that they can breathe.

Plants use the carbon dioxide that people and animals breathe out.

How do plants live?

Green plants make their own food. They soak up water and minerals from the soil which goes up the stems to the leaves.

In the leaves, sunlight helps water and carbon dioxide from the air to make sugar. Sugar is food for plants.

Animals and people move around to find food. Plants make their own. They spend their whole lives in one place.

From seed to seed

Caterpillars, slugs and snails like to eat young shoots.

Most plants grow from seeds. A sunflower seed rests until rain makes it swell. A root grows down into the soil and a shoot pushes up towards the light.

At first, the plant gets all its food from the seed, but once proper leaves grow they make food for the plant. Then the plant grows a flower bud.

The flower opens and is soon pollinated. New seeds grow, ripen and fall to the ground. Those that survive grow into flowers the following year.

Why do plants have flowers?

Flowers are the part of the plant where seeds are made. Most flowers have bright petals and a sweet scent.

To make the seeds, a fine yellow dust called pollen has to be carried from one flower to another. Insects, or the wind, do this job.

Flowers produce a sweet liquid called nectar which many insects like to drink. The flowers' colour and scent draw them to the nectar.

As an insect drinks, pollen sticks to its body. When the insect visits another flower this pollen rubs off onto it and pollinates it.

How seeds leave plants

When seeds are ripe, they leave the plant to grow in a new place. Many are blown away by the wind or carried by water.

Some seeds stick to the coats or feet of birds and animals. Later on they fall off and grow where they land.

Other seeds grow inside pods which ripen in the Sun and burst open, hurling the seeds away from the parent plant.

Trappers, stranglers and pricklers

Venus fly trap plants eat insects for extra nutrients. Their leaves snap shut when an insect lands.

Some plants are parasites and feed off living plants. They have no roots in the ground.

Other plants have prickles or can sting, which helps to protect them from birds or animals.

Trees and habitats

Trees cover about a third of the Earth's land surface. They are the largest living things and live longer than anything else.

The tallest tree on record is a redwood tree in America called 'Tallest Tree'. It is 112.1 metres high.

The oldest tree on record was a bristlecone pine in America. It was 4,000 years old when it was cut down.

Why trees lose their leaves

Trees called evergreens can keep each leaf for several years. Deciduous trees lose all their leaves every year.

In the autumn, deciduous trees lose their leaves to protect them from the cold and frost in the winter.

A corky layer grows across each leaf stalk. Water cannot reach the leaves, so they die. New leaves grow in the spring.

How old is a tree?

Every year a layer of wood grows inside the trunk and makes a ring. The number of rings on a tree trunk tells you how old the tree is. They also tell you the tree's life story.

1. The wide even rings mean this tree grew quickly at first.

2. It was nearly knocked over, but grew more quickly on one side to straighten itself.

3. For a while the tree was crowded by others. The thin rings show that this made it grow slowly.

6. Narrow rings show there was a drought one year.

5. These are fire scars from a forest fire.

4. The trees around were cut down and the tree had more room so it grew more quickly again.

44

The tree house

Many things can live in and around a tree. They all live alongside each other. Each of them has a place of its own so that they do not have to compete for the food and shelter a tree gives them.

Great spotted woodpeckers chip away the bark and eat the insects beneath it.

The lichen moth hides on the tree. Its wings look the same as the lichen growing on the tree trunk.

These grey squirrels live in a leafy nest, called a drey, where they look after their young.

The long-eared bat hangs in the hollow trunk and sleeps during the day.

Plants like this ivy climb up trees to get more light.

Earthworms eat dead leaves which fall off the trees. Moles tunnel to catch the worms.

Tawny Owl

Blue Tit

Acorn Weevil

Fox and Cubs

Rabbits

Toad

Violets

Wild Bees

Speckled Wood Butterfly

Hedgehog

Badger

Shrew

Worms

Mole

45

Insects

There are over a million different kinds of insect and they live everywhere in the world, except in deep sea water. They usually have six legs, a pair of feelers, one or two pairs of wings and a body divided into three parts.

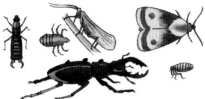

Spiders are not insects

Spiders belong to a group of animals called arachnids. Unlike insects, they have eight legs and no wings. There are only two parts to their bodies and they usually have eight eyes.

Parts of a fly

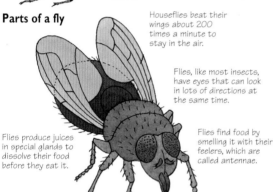

Houseflies beat their wings about 200 times a minute to stay in the air.

Flies, like most insects, have eyes that can look in lots of directions at the same time.

Flies produce juices in special glands to dissolve their food before they eat it.

Flies find food by smelling it with their feelers, which are called antennae.

The house fly can walk upside down because it has sticky pads under the claws on its feet.

They have tongue-like mouth parts which they use to get the food ready to eat.

Biters and suckers

Not all insects feed in the same way. Wasps and beetles can bite things and have strong jaws and sharp teeth.

Mosquitoes drink human or animal blood by sucking it up through their needle-like mouth parts. Some carry diseases.

Hide and seek

Some insects look like plants. This camouflages them so that neither their prey, nor their enemies, can see them.

Some insects mimic others to confuse their enemies. Birds leave the harmless hornet moth alone mistaking it for the dangerous stinging hornet.

Wasps and bees have poisonous stings to defend themselves. Most birds and other animals do not like to eat them.

The four stages of a butterfly

After a female butterfly has mated, she lays her eggs on a plant and dies. A caterpillar hatches from each egg and begins to eat.

As it eats, it outgrows its skin and grows a new one. When it is fully grown, its skin hardens to form a chrysalis. Changes begin to take place inside it.

Inside the chrysalis, the caterpillar slowly changes into a butterfly. Then it pulls itself out of the chrysalis and flies away.

Inside the palace

A single honey bee cannot survive on its own for long. Bees live in hives along with as many as 80,000 other bees.

Every hive has one queen bee, thousands of worker bees and several hundred male bees which are called drones.

Dancing the waggle

All the bees eat honey. They make it from flower nectar and keep it in six-sided wax cells called honeycomb.

Bees dance to tell each other where to find nectar. A circular dance means it is near by. A waggle dance means it is further away.

The queen bee lays all the eggs but she cannot look after them. Some of the eggs hatch into drones, whose job is to fertilize eggs.

At first worker bees build and clean the hive.

Later they feed the grubs that emerge from the eggs. The grubs will grow into bees.

Older worker bees go out in search of nectar and pollen.

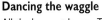

When there are too many bees in a hive, a second queen flies away with a swarm of workers and starts a new hive.

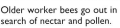
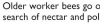

Life in the ocean

Life at the bottom

Many fish and other sea creatures live in the shallow water near the shore. The shells on the beach were once the homes of some of them. Crabs search the seashore for food at high tide.

Seaweed

There are also many different kinds of sea plants. Their long stems float in the water and instead of roots, they have sucker pads which they fasten onto rocks.

Limpets move about on a fleshy foot, but always return to the same place on a rock.

Sea anemones paralyse small fish with their tentacles, then they feed on them.

If a starfish has an arm bitten off by an enemy, it can grow a new one.

Fish facts

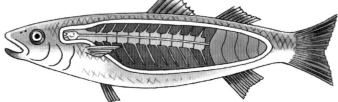

Many fish have good eyesight. They do not have eyelids as the sea keeps their eyes moist and clean.

Fish have a good sense of smell. They smell through their nostrils, but they do not breathe through them.

Fish use their fins for cornering, balancing, braking and steering. They use their tails to drive themselves along.

Food of the sea

Plankton are minute animals and plants that drift close to the surface of the water. They are the main food of many sea creatures.

Sometimes there can be so much plankton in the water the sea turns green or red.

Life on the surface

Most fish live near the surface of the water. These fish never stop swimming and their streamlined shapes help them to swim fast.

Life in the dark

No sunlight reaches the depths of the ocean. Few fish live there and those that do often produce lights to lure prey and attract mates.

Flying fish can travel 100 metres through the air.

The enormous whale shark lives entirely on plankton.

The giant squid's enemy is the sperm whale. They battle in the depths of the ocean.

Scientists thought coelacanths had died out 70 million years ago, but in 1938 one was found deep in the Indian Ocean.

Like people, fish need oxygen to breathe, but they get it from water. As a fish swallows, water passes over its gills.

The gills strain the oxygen from the water and then force it out through gill covers behind the fish's eyes.

Most fish have babies by laying eggs. Some of them build nests but others lay them straight into the water.

Reptiles

Alligators, crocodiles, tortoises, turtles, snakes and lizards are all members of the reptile family.

Reptiles live mainly on land, but some of them spend a lot of time in water. They all have scaly, watertight skins.

They are cold-blooded which means that the temperature of their bodies is always the same as that of their surroundings.

Most reptiles are carnivorous. This means that they eat other animals. Some of them can swallow their prey whole.

Reptiles lay eggs

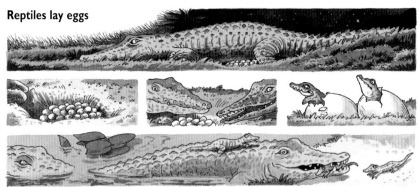

After she has mated, the female crocodile digs a hole at night and lays about forty eggs. Both parents guard them carefully.

In about 90 days the young crocodiles hatch. Crocodiles carry their babies around in their jaws to keep them safe.

The babies can feed themselves straightaway, but their parents still keep watch over them until they are really strong.

Dealing with enemies

Some snakes kill their prey with a poisonous bite. Others, such as the boa constrictor, squeeze their prey to death.

Tortoises and turtles draw back into the safety of their hard shells if they are frightened or in any kind of danger.

Some lizards have tails that break off when they want to escape from an enemy. A new tail grows in its place.

Amphibians

What is an amphibian?

Frogs, toads, newts, salamanders and worm-like animals, called caecilians, are all types of amphibian.

They are called amphibians because they live both in water and on land. They only need water to breed in.

Amphibians have backbones and are cold-blooded. Most of them breathe through their skins, but some have lungs.

Frogs

Like all amphibians, frogs lay their eggs in water. The eggs are called 'frog spawn' and look like tiny balls of jelly.

After about two weeks tiny tadpoles hatch. They eat leaves with their horny lips and teeth, and breathe through their gills, like fish.

Two small bumps appear on their tails which grow into back legs. At about ten weeks old, tadpoles grow forelegs and their tails become shorter.

After about three months, they look like tiny frogs. They can leap out of the water and breathe air. Every day they hunt for insects to eat.

Other amphibians

The fire salamander has a deadly form of protection. It oozes poison from its skin to warn animals not to eat it.

An axolotl is a type of salamander. Unlike most other amphibians, it breeds and spends its whole life in water.

Some toads that live in the Australian desert survive in dry weather by storing rainwater in their bodies.

51

Birds

What are birds?

There are about 8,600 different kinds of bird in the world. Birds are warm-blooded, like us. They have backbones and are the only creatures with feathers.

All birds have wings and most of them can fly. Birds which cannot fly, such as the African ostrich, have strong legs so that they can run fast to escape from their enemies.

How do birds fly?

Birds twist or bend their wings to change direction. Their streamlined shapes help them to fly fast.

Birds are very light because their bones are hollow, and because there are air spaces throughout their bodies.

When birds take off, they leap into the air and flap their wings very quickly.

Some large birds are so heavy, they have to run and flap their wings to gain enough speed to take off.

Large birds spread their wings and flap them slowly. They glide on currents of air, searching the ground for food.

Small birds flap their wings very fast. Hummingbirds can hover in one place, and fly backwards and forwards.

Migrating birds

Some birds migrate. This means they fly away to a warm place every autumn where there is plenty of food to eat.

Some birds fly by day and others by night. No one knows how birds find their way. They may use the Sun and the stars.

Arctic terns fly the greatest distance. They fly across the world from the Arctic to the Antarctic and back each year.

Beaks and birds of prey

Birds cannot chew because they have no teeth. They swallow their food whole. It is ground up in part of their stomach, called the gizzard.

You can tell what a bird eats by the shape of its beak. Pelicans catch fish in their baggy beaks. Flamingoes can sieve food out of mud with their beaks.

Birds of prey have curved talons which they use to stun and grab small animals and birds. They have large, hooked beaks for tearing up the flesh.

Feathers

Feathers trap more air so they are warmer than fur. Birds fluff up their feathers on cold days to trap as much air as possible.

Birds clean, tidy and oil their feathers. The oil comes from a gland above the tail and keeps the feathers waterproof.

Feathers become ragged and worn after a while. At least once a year they drop out, or moult, and new ones grow.

Nesting

Male birds have to attract a mate. Some birds have one partner for life. Others find a new mate every nesting season.

Some birds show off their colours or preen their feathers to attract a mate. Others put on a flying display or perform dances.

All birds lay eggs, usually in a hidden nest. The female bird, and sometimes the male, sits on the eggs to keep them warm.

Chicks hatched in nests above the ground are usually naked and helpless. Their parents feed them until they can fly properly.

Chicks hatched on the ground are covered with fluffy down. They can run and peck things to eat when they hatch.

Mammals

There are about 4,500 kinds of mammal. All the animals on these pages are mammals. So are human beings.

Mammals are the only animals with hair or fur. Some grow a thicker, warmer coat in the cold winter months.

Mammals are warm-blooded. This means that their bodies stay the same temperature whatever the weather outside.

Moving about

Most land mammals have four legs. Sea mammals, such as sea-lions and dolphins, have flippers instead of legs.

Kangaroos hop about on their hind legs, which are very strong. Their long tails help them to balance.

Bats are the only mammals which can fly. They use their arms as wings. The skin is stretched over the bones.

Protection

Mammals protect themselves from danger in different ways. Some of them can run away fast. Others have prickly coats to protect them. Skunks make a very nasty smell.

Many jungle and forest mammals have markings on their coats to camouflage them from their enemies and prey. They match the colours and patterns on trees and undergrowth.

Living together

Some mammals, such as chimpanzees, are very sociable and live together in groups. The females look after the young and the males defend the group from their enemies.

Lions live in a group called a pride. The lionesses do most of the hunting and feed and care for the cubs. The male lions keep watch of the pride's territory.

Mammals are the only animals which produce milk to feed their new-born babies. Some feed lots of babies at once.

Many mammals are intelligent and curious. They can learn how to do new and different things.

All of them breathe air. Even a whale, which spends its whole life in water, comes to the surface to breathe.

Most mammals build homes to keep them dry, safe and warm. Some of them spend the whole winter asleep in their homes, such as the polar bear, which digs a cave out of snow and ice.

Beavers build their homes in rivers and streams with sticks and mud. Their homes, called lodges, have underwater entrances. They have separate living and sleeping areas.

Baby mammals

Many mammals have more than one mate. Each year male red deer mate with a group of females.

Some babies take longer than others to grow inside their mothers. Mice take three weeks, human babies take nine months.

When they are born, the babies feed on their mother's milk. This has everything the baby needs to grow.

Some mothers stay with their babies for longer than others. They all stay until the babies can look after themselves.

Baby kangaroos are born before they are fully formed. They finish growing inside their mother's warm pouch.

The platypus and the spiny anteater are two unusual mammals as they lay eggs. Their eggs have soft shells.

The human body

How do we stand up?

There are about 206 bones in the human body. They are all linked together by joints to make a skeleton. Without this you would just be a mound of flesh.

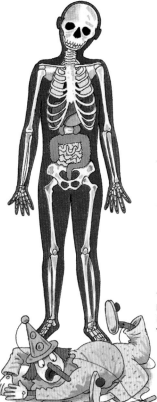

Bones protect vital parts of the body, such as the heart and lungs, from damage. The brain is protected by 30 skull bones all tightly locked together.

How bones are joined together

A joint is where two bones meet. Most bones move at the joint. Some move backwards and forwards like a hinge.

Others are called ball and socket joints. These allow the bones to move in many different directions.

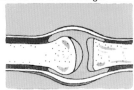

Joints contain a fluid which keeps them oiled and easy to move. Straps, called ligaments, hold the bones in place.

Some people can bend their joints more than other people because they have very loose ligaments.

Why you can move

You can move because your bones are attached to muscles. Every joint has two muscles which work in turn.

To make a bone move, a message from your brain tells one muscle to pull on the bone and the other to relax.

Overworked muscles produce a poison which makes you feel tired. Blood washes it away and you feel better.

Your heart is another type of muscle. It works by itself without stopping for the whole of your life.

56

What happens to the food you eat?

You grind up food with your teeth and it mixes with saliva in your mouth. This helps it to slide down to your stomach.

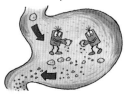

Special juices in your stomach start to break the food down into tiny bits. This is called digestion.

The digested food enters the bloodstream through a wiggly tube called the small intestine, and goes all around your body.

Waste goes into a tube, called the large intestine, and gets ready to leave the body. Other waste is removed as the blood passes through the kidneys.

How blood goes round

Your heart is a pump. It pumps blood through one tube and sucks it in through another.

Blood flows around your body through rubbery tubes. Laid end to end, they would go nearly half way to the Moon.

Tubes called arteries take blood away from the heart. It turns red when it collects oxygen from the lungs.

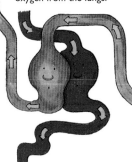

Used blood returns to the heart in tubes called veins. It looks purple because the oxygen has been used up.

What does blood do?

Blood carries tiny bits of food to your liver. The liver sorts the food out so that it is ready for your body to use.

Your blood fights germs that get into your body and could make you ill. It surrounds them and then kills them.

Blood carries the oxygen you breathe in around your body. It takes waste gas to your lungs for you to breathe out.

When you hurt yourself, your blood makes special gluey stuff which blocks wounds and stops them bleeding.

The human body

What happens when you breathe?

You can live for several days without food, but only a few minutes without air.

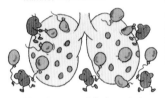

Your lungs are full of tiny holes, like sponges, and many blood vessels. The oxygen in the air passes into your blood.

When you breathe in, the air goes down your windpipe into your two lungs.

Dust and dirt in the air are trapped by tiny hairs in your nose, so they do not go down into your lungs.

How do your lungs work?

As you breathe in, your ribs move up and out. A muscle under your lungs, called a diaphragm, flattens down. Air rushes in to fill your lungs.

When you breathe out, your ribs drop back. Your diaphragm pops up. All the used gases are squeezed out.

Making sense

You have five senses. They tell you what is happening around your body by sending messages to your brain.

Hearing

When your ears hear this sound your memory says 'music'.

Sight

Your eyes see the clock and your memory says '7.30'.

Smell

Your nose smells cooking and your memory says 'cake'.

Taste

Your tongue tastes the drink and your memory says 'milk'.

Touch

You feel with the skin on your fingers. Your memory works out who or what it is.

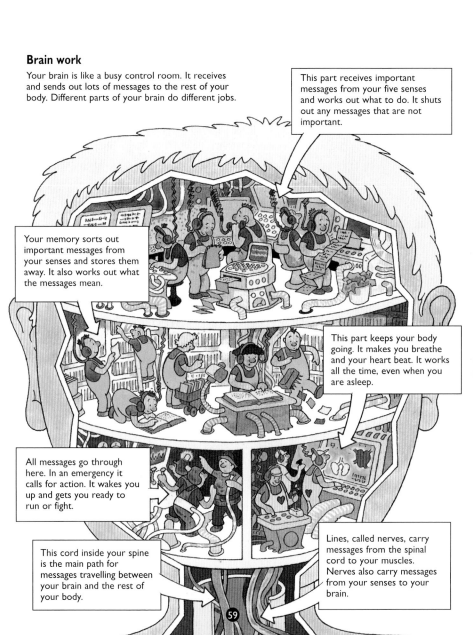

Brain work

Your brain is like a busy control room. It receives and sends out lots of messages to the rest of your body. Different parts of your brain do different jobs.

This part receives important messages from your five senses and works out what to do. It shuts out any messages that are not important.

Your memory sorts out important messages from your senses and stores them away. It also works out what the messages mean.

This part keeps your body going. It makes you breathe and your heart beat. It works all the time, even when you are asleep.

All messages go through here. In an emergency it calls for action. It wakes you up and gets you ready to run or fight.

This cord inside your spine is the main path for messages travelling between your brain and the rest of your body.

Lines, called nerves, carry messages from the spinal cord to your muscles. Nerves also carry messages from your senses to your brain.

Looking after the land

Rainforests cover an area about the size of the United States. More than half the world's types of animals and birds live in these forests.

But thousands of them all over the world are in danger of dying out because the rainforests are being cut down and destroyed by humans.

People chop down the trees so that they can sell the valuable wood for money. Others clear the land to grow crops for food.

When forests are cut and burnt, the animals and birds lose their homes and food. If there are no other trees to move to, they starve and die.

Making deserts

Many people clear forests to grow grass for their cattle. If the animals eat all the grass the land becomes desert.

The loss of the forests is likely to alter the world's climate, causing droughts and changes in wind and rainfall.

Many of the things we use come from rainforests, such as medicines, rubber, oils, spices and perfumes.

Poisoning the Earth

People destroy plants, birds and animals when they tip poisonous wastes, such as oil, into rivers, lakes and seas.

Untreated sewage in seas and rivers may spread diseases and also kill fish, by rotting and so using up oxygen in the water.

Fumes from factories and car exhausts pollute the air. They make it harmful to breathe and kill plants and trees.

Farming the land

Soil is full of minerals and elements that plants need to grow. Without these things the land is bare and lifeless.

If soil is overused, healthy plants cannot grow in it. Good farmers put back in the soil the minerals that the crops use up.

Not all plants use up the same things from the soil. Farmers give the soil a rest by growing different crops each season.

Tree roots help to keep the soil in place. They stop it from being blown away by the wind or washed away by the rain.

Some farmers build terrace walls to stop steep land from slipping away and to make more flat land for them to farm.

Others plant hedges around fields to protect the land from the wind. Many birds and animals make their homes in hedges.

A safe life in the wild

Many countries set up nature reserves where animals can live safely in their natural habitat. People can visit them there.

Wildlife moves to town

A few animals, such as foxes, have moved from their natural home in the country to live in towns, where food is easier to find.

The story of people

Millions of years ago

Our early ancestors were probably ape-like creatures who were much smaller than us.

Between 6 and 4.5 million years ago, a very early type of human being, called a hominid, had begun to walk upright.

They ate plants, berries and raw animal meat. About 2.3 million years ago, they were learning how to make stone tools.

Wandering hunters

50,000BC

Village farmers

10,000BC

Our direct ancestors appeared at this time. They lived in caves, hunted animals with stone weapons, and could make fire.

In the Middle East people collected wild seeds and grew crops. The first farm animals were tamed wild animals.

The people built mud houses and settled down to farm the land. They made clay pots and learned how to weave cloth.

The first cities

5000BC to 2000BC

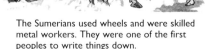

The Sumerians in the Middle East built villages which grew into huge walled cities. They had a temple in the centre.

The Sumerians used wheels and were skilled metal workers. They were one of the first peoples to write things down.

The Ancient World

3100BC to 1500BC

500BC to 140BC

The Ancient Egyptians used a calendar like ours. They designed the water clock and could make paper. Their kings, called pharaohs, were often buried in pyramids when they died.

The Ancient Greeks were great sculptors, writers and doctors. Greek citizens were the first people to help govern their cities by voting on important matters.

750BC to AD500

Dates with BC after them are the number of years before the birth of Christ counting backwards. Dates with AD are the number of years after the birth of Christ.

BC ⟵ ⟶ AD

The Romans had very large armies. They conquered Europe, North Africa, and the Middle East.

Their engineers built fine roads and bridges across the Empire. They also built many towns and cities, and set up trade routes.

The Middle Ages

AD1000 to AD1450

In the Middle Ages each of the different countries of Europe was ruled by a king or emperor who owned all the land.

When the king wanted money or soldiers, he met his most important subjects. This idea led to the first parliament.

The Renaissance

AD1450 to AD1750

At this time, Europeans took an interest in the art and learning of Ancient Greece and Rome.

They did lots of scientific and medical experiments to find out more about the world.

The Industrial Revolution

AD1750 to AD1914

New machines were invented which did many of the jobs people used to do by hand.

Modern times

Electronic inventions have changed people's lives much faster than ever before.

Clues to the past

For thousands of years different people have lived on the same site, leaving behind all sorts of remains. Scientists dig these up to discover clues to our history.

A living thing, such as a tree, absorbs radioactive carbon or C14. When it dies, C14 slowly leaves the tree. Scientists can calculate how old the wood is from the amount of C14 left.

You can read more about some of these people on pages 64 to 75. 63

Cave people

Our direct ancestors were cave people who appeared 50,000 years ago, during the last Ice Age, and spread all over the world.

They are also known as hunter-gatherers, as they hunted animals with stone weapons, caught fish and gathered nuts, seeds, berries and roots.

Tent life

Some groups hunted away from the caves on the bare, frozen plains of Eastern Europe. They lived in tents.

The tents were made of animal skins, raised over shallow pits with low stone walls. Bones or tusks held them up.

A large tent could house several families. Each family had its own fireplace for heating and cooking.

Dressing up

Cave people were the first people to sew. They made clothes by stitching skins together with bone needles.

Sometimes they decorated their clothes with little beads of coloured rock or shells with holes in them.

They wore necklaces and bracelets made of teeth, beads, ivory and stone threaded together with leather strips.

Decorating the cave

Cave people painted pictures on their cave walls of the animals they hunted. Their paints were made from powdered rock.

To give themselves light, these early people used lamps of burning fur or moss, soaked in animal fat.

They carved stone pictures of pregnant women. This may have been to bring them good fortune.

Preparing for the hunt

The hunters made their axes, knives and spears out of pieces of flint which they chipped into shape and sharpened.

When they spotted a herd of animals, they planned the best way to chase and catch them, without anyone getting hurt.

Sometimes they made traps. They dug pits, filled them with sharpened stakes, then covered them with branches.

The kill

The greatest prey of all for hunters was the giant woolly mammoth, as it provided them with everything they needed.

They followed the mammoth and then closed in for the kill with their spears. Sometimes they chased it into a bog, so it could not fight back.

The hunters skinned the mammoth, and carried pieces of meat and bones back to the camp.

If a wounded hunter died, he was buried in the floor of the cave with his jewellery and weapons.

Then they covered him with a red ochre powder and laid mammoth bones or flowers on his grave.

Ancient Egyptians

The Ancient Egyptians lived between the years 4000BC and 500BC, in the dry, hot country along the River Nile.

Every July, the river flooded and the farmers grew their crops in rich, fertile mud which the flood left behind.

It was a serious crime either to block the channels of water to a farmer's field, or to move his boundary stones.

A rich noble lived in this house made of sun dried mud bricks, with a wooden roof.

The walls and mud floors were painted and often hung with reed mats.

The family slept at the back, or in the summer, on the roof. They had a bathroom and a lavatory.

Cool clothes and make-up

Egyptians wore cool clothes made of linen. The men wore short tunics and the women wore long tunics with shoulder straps.

Both men and women wore make-up. Rich people wore wigs and jewellery made from gold and semi-precious stones.

In hot weather, children often wore no clothes. Boys had shaved heads with a single lock of hair. Girls wore several plaits.

Feasts and fun

Rich people had grand parties with lots of food and drink, served by servants and slaves.

A cone of scented fat was put on each guest's head. As it melted, it covered them with scent.

The guests were entertained by singers, dancers, acrobats, jugglers and musicians.

Sports and games

The Egyptians hunted on land from chariots and in water from boats. Here they are catching a hippopotamus with harpoons and ropes.

The children played with leather balls and toys made of wood and ivory. They enjoyed wrestling and fencing with wooden swords.

Education

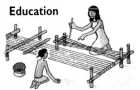

Most children did not go to school. Boys learned their father's trade and girls helped their mothers.

Rich children had a tutor or went to school. They learned to read and write on paper made from papyrus reeds.

They used picture writing called hieroglyphics. Sometimes a picture stood for a sound and several pictures made a word.

The burial of a king

Egyptian kings built huge stone pyramids in the desert as their burial places.

Men spent part of each year working on buildings for the king, as tax payment.

When the king died, his body was preserved and wrapped in linen. This was called a mummy.

The king was buried seventy days after death. His funeral procession included priests, priestesses and paid mourners.

Inside the tomb were clothes, weapons, furniture and anything else the king needed for his life after death.

Sometimes robbers would try to break into the sealed tomb and steal the treasures which were buried with the king.

The Ancient Romans

The Ancient Romans lived between about 750BC and AD500. Rome grew up on seven hills near the River Tiber.

Romans were either citizens or non-citizens. Citizens had certain rights, such as a say in the government, and were protected by laws.

Many Romans had slaves. As the Roman Empire grew, thousands of prisoners were taken and sold at slave markets.

A Roman street

Most Romans rented rooms in blocks of flats. Many did not have kitchens because of the danger of catching fire.

In Rome there were several markets. Other towns just had one which was held once a week in the main square.

Water was piped into the city and Romans collected it from public fountains. Underground pipes carried away the waste.

People bought hot food and drink from eating houses and street stalls. They drank wine and talked in the taverns.

The shops opened onto the street and had a counter at the front. Slaves often did the shopping for their owners.

Pavements were built higher than the roads. People used stepping stones to cross the road in wet weather.

Only rich people could afford a whole house to themselves. They stuck bits of coloured stone on the floor to make pictures, called mosaics.

Wealthy Romans lay on couches for meals. They used their fingers to eat from big dishes. Some of them went on eating until they were sick.

Washing and dressing

Roman citizens liked to visit the public baths. The steam baths and hot pools were heated by an underground furnace. They also played games and met their friends there.

Men who were citizens wore a tunic and a piece of cloth wrapped round their body, called a toga. The women wore a dress called a stola, with a shawl over the top.

School and play

Only the children of rich parents went to school. Some were taught at home by private tutors or educated slaves. They learnt to write on wax tablets and did sums on an abacus.

Keeping fit was important, so when lessons were over, the boys ran, wrestled and fenced. Boys and girls liked to play games such as rolling hoops and throwing knucklebones like dice.

The Roman army

The army was very well trained and conquered a great deal of land for the Roman Empire. So the Roman way of life spread.

When attacking the enemy, the army used catapults that hurled heavy rocks, and battering rams to knock down walls.

Roman foot soldiers were each given a bronze helmet, a shield, a breastplate, short sword and a long spear.

Games

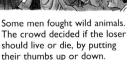

On public holidays or to celebrate a victory, great fights and chariot races were held to entertain everyone.

Men, called gladiators, were taught to fight and die bravely. They were often slaves, criminals or men in debt.

Some men fought wild animals. The crowd decided if the loser should live or die, by putting their thumbs up or down.

The Middle Ages

Between about AD1000 and AD1450 each country in Europe was ruled by a king who owned all the land.

The king gave land to his supporters and made them nobles. In return they promised to fight for him.

Workers, called villeins, farmed the nobles' land. They paid rent and gave the nobles part of their crops.

Castle life

Kings and nobles built castles to protect themselves against their enemies. Armed soldiers kept watch day and night.

Training to be a knight

A noble's son trained to be a knight. First, he was a pageboy in a noble's family. They taught him how to behave well.

Next, he worked as a squire, the servant of a knight. He learned about armour, weapons and riding.

Sometimes the lord held feasts in the great hall. All the family and important guests sat at the top table.

Minstrels played music to the guests. Often leftover food was collected and given to the local poor people.

A squire was made a knight by his lord when he had proved he was brave. Knights were called 'Sir'.

Village life

Most people lived in villages. Their small houses had thatched roofs with a hole in, to let the smoke out.

The people worked in the fields every day except on holy days and on Sundays, when they went to the village church.

Villagers could graze their cattle on 'common land'. Stray animals were locked up until their owners paid a fine.

Women spun wool from their sheep and sold it to travelling merchants who then had it woven into cloth.

If a person committed a small crime they might be put in the stocks as punishment and the villagers threw things at them.

At the village fair

Traders bought goods from the villagers and sold them goods from other villages and abroad.

Tinkers sold pots and pans. Jugglers and musicians entertained the crowd.

The runaway villein

A villein who wanted his freedom had to run away from the village and avoid being caught for a year and a day.

If he went to a town he could learn a trade. He had to work for several years as apprentice to a craftsman.

The Black Death

In AD1348 some sailors arrived in Italy, from Asia, with a terrible disease called the Black Death.

The disease spread across Europe carried by the fleas on rats. About one person in every three died of it.

The Industrial Revolution

The time between 1750 and 1914 is called the Industrial Revolution. This is because so many machines were invented which changed people's lives.

Before that time there were few big towns. Most people lived in the countryside. They farmed their own land or worked for the local landowner.

Some people made money from spinning and weaving wool in their homes. They sold it to travelling merchants.

The power of machines

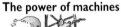

Then, machines that were driven by steam engines were invented. They could make cloth very quickly.

Factories were built for the new machines and many people moved to the towns to work in the factories.

Coal was needed to run the machines. Children worked in the mines, hauling coal to the surface on underground rails.

The daily grind

Both children and adults worked in the factories for six days a week. The work was hard and the hours were very long.

They often worked from six in the morning till eight at night. They were paid very little and the work was sometimes dangerous.

Life in the towns

The factory owners became very rich and lived well, but the factory workers were very poor. They lived in tiny, crowded houses with no bathroom or clean water.

People who lost their jobs often had to go and live in the 'workhouse' where they were given food and a bed in return for work. Families were separated and life was hard.

Room for improvement

At last laws were made to improve people's lives. Better houses were built and free schools set up for all children.

In some countries, people without jobs were given a small amount of money to support themselves.

Workers joined together to form trade unions, so they could bargain for better wages and working conditions.

Going further faster

Roads and bridges were built so that people and goods could move about more easily. Everyone paid a small fee, called a toll, to use them.

People realised that it was cheaper to move heavy goods, such as coal, by boat. So a huge network of canals was built.

The new steam trains carried people and goods further and faster than ever before. More families went away on holiday.

There was more trade between countries around the world as travel by steam ships became more reliable, faster and cheaper.

Modern times

The way people live and travel has changed far more over the last hundred years than ever before in history.

Two world wars caused social changes. Women now have the right to vote, and many do jobs that only men did in the past.

Modern medicine and better living conditions mean that people live longer today than they used to in the past.

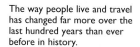

Vast networks of roads, railways, ships and aeroplanes link all the world's countries.

Space probes explore the universe and send information back to Earth.

The United States of America has enough road to go around the world over 150 times.

In 1969, Neil Armstrong, an American astronaut, was the first person to walk on the Moon.

Jumbo jets fly from Britain to Australia in about 20 hours. Sailing ships took six months.

Keeping in touch

News often took weeks or months to reach people in the past. Now they receive news by television, radio and newspapers every day.

Many satellites orbit the Earth. They flash information, television pictures and thousands of telephone calls all around the world.

Fast food and gadgets

Many people do their shopping in giant supermarkets. The food is often already weighed, measured and wrapped.

Refrigerators keep food fresh. Food can be deep frozen so that it can travel long distances and be sold all over the world.

Housework is much easier and faster than ever before because of the many electrical gadgets people can buy to help them.

City life

About a third of the people in the world live in towns and cities. Most cities have very tall buildings because of the shortage of land.

Machine work

Machines now do a lot of the work that people used to do.

Computers are programmed to copy human thinking. They can solve some problems faster than a person.

This robot has arms that can piece things together on a factory production line.

Students use machines such as computers, tape recorders, calculators and videos to help them learn.

Fame and fortune

Musicians and film stars can become world famous overnight as their discs, videos and movies are sold all around the world.

Every four years the best athletes in the world compete against each other at the Olympic Games to try to beat world records.

People around the world

There are many different races of people all over the world. Each race has its own customs, culture and religion.

Nowadays, fast modern travel has made it easy for people from different countries to meet and learn about each other.

Tallest and smallest

The tallest people in the world are the African Watussi tribe. Most of the men are over 183 cms.

The smallest people also live in Africa. The Mbuti pygmies are only about 132 cms.

There are still primitive tribes living like Stone Age people in places like the Amazon jungle.

Different races of people have different looks and builds. They probably developed these to help them survive in the part of the world in which they lived.

People living in cloudy climates may originally have had pale skins. This helped them get the vitamins they needed from the Sun.

Black skin and thick curly hair probably helped protect people from the Sun in hot, dry places.

People who lived in very cold conditions may have developed narrow eyes and flat noses to protect them from the cold.

There are now about 6,000 million people in the world, and each year, there are 90 million more people.

Languages

People are different from animals because they are able to speak to each other.

Learning to speak

Usually the first language a person learns to speak is called their 'mother tongue' or native language.

In countries where many languages are spoken, there is usually one official language which is used in schools.

1000 million Mandarin
350 million English

China's official language is Mandarin. Over 1000 million people speak it, which is more than any other language.

Language families

There are 10,000 different languages. Many of them came from a single language.

If a language is related to another, it belongs to the same 'language' family.

FRENCH   SPANISH

French, Spanish and Italian all grew from the Latin language.

LATIN

ITALIAN

Some Eastern languages, such as Japanese, are completely different from any other.

Spreading the word

As groups of people moved from one part of the world to another, they took their language with them. In time, they began to say words in a slightly different way.

They made up new words for foreign things that they had never seen before.

Gradually a language may change so much that it becomes a new one.

Houses and homes

All over the world, people build houses for shelter and protection. They use materials that are easy to come by.

In the Kalahari Desert in Africa, some San people still build huts with grasses and branches.

People also build houses to suit the climate. In hot, wet places, houses are built on stilts to keep them cool and dry.

Nomads are people who move from place to place, herding their animals. They carry their tents with them.

In cities, many people live in high rise flats. This way, more homes can be built on one piece of land.

People experiment with new types of houses. This inflatable home is useful in emergencies such as a flood or earthquake.

Houses in the heat

Many villages in Africa, such as the Nabdam houses in northern Ghana, are built of mud baked hard by the Sun. The thick walls block out the Sun and keep the inside cool. The houses are painted on the outside with vegetable juices.

In the steamy Amazon jungle, Yanomamo Indians build huge circular roofs with palm tree leaves laid over wooden poles. As there are no walls they store their few belongings off the ground to keep them dry.

Houses in the cold

In Switzerland, houses called chalets are built of wood. The ground floor is made of stone which does not rot in the damp, and the windows have double layers of glass. Snow settles on the sloping roof and helps to keep the heat in.

Nowadays in Lapland most people live in small towns beyond the Arctic Circle. However, there are some reindeer herdsmen who live in tents. These are made from large branches covered in reindeer skins.

A travelling house

The Bedouins are Arabs who wander across the Arabian desert herding their animals.

They live in goat hair tents woven by the women. Each tent has a dividing curtain.

On one side the family sleep and cook. On the other, men entertain guests.

A floating house

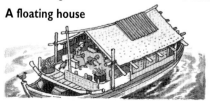

Many people in China cook, eat and sleep on houseboats called sampans. They also keep chicken and grow vegetables on board.

Living together

A kibbutz is a type of village in Israel where everyone shares in the work and land, and has a say in how things are organized.

Food and cooking

Everything you eat and drink affects your body in some way. Food is vital as it gives you energy to keep going. Without food you would not be able to grow, move about, keep warm or get better when you are ill. You need lots of different sorts of food to stay healthy.

People can survive for several weeks without food but only a few days without water.

Vegetables, fruit and milk provide the important vitamins and minerals your body needs.

Protein foods, such as meat, fish and milk build your body.

Starchy foods such as bread and cereals give you energy.

Your body can store fats from butters and oils and use them later for energy.

Feast or famine?

Nearly half the people in the world are starving because their crops have been destroyed by drought.

There is enough food in the world for everybody, but the great problem is sending it to where it is most needed.

Eating too much, and eating too many fatty and sugary foods can make people overweight, unhealthy and even ill.

Fast foods

Why do people cook?

Fast foods are quick and cheap to cook. Some contain a lot of fat and sugar and are bad for you if you eat too much of them.

Cooked food is easier for your stomach to digest than raw food. Cooking kills germs that may make people ill, and makes food keep longer.

Everyday food

The main food of a country is called its 'staple food'. Rice is the staple food of half the world. It only grows in warm climates.

The biggest meal in the world

Roast camel stuffed with sheep, chickens, fish and eggs is the largest meal in the world. It is served at Bedouin weddings in Africa.

Meals around the world

This Indian family roasts meat, such as lamb or chicken, in a clay oven called a tandoor. The name 'tandoori' is given to meat dishes cooked this way. Most Indians do not eat beef.

They serve their meat with vegetables, pickles, and bread called chapattis, and eat it with their fingers. Spices are used to flavour the food and make it tasty.

Chinese families cook their food over a fire in shallow metal pans, called woks. They eat rice with vegetables and a little meat.

The food is eaten out of small bowls using wooden sticks, called chopsticks. They drink milkless tea with their meals.

This Italian family begins a meal with a plate of pasta served with a sauce. Italians eat a lot of pasta, which they make in different shapes with wheat flour and water.

Next, they have meat and vegetables, which they eat with knives and forks. They drink wine with their meal. The children drink a little wine mixed with water.

Sport

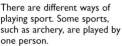

People of all ages enjoy sport. Some people like restful sports and others prefer to be active or competitive.

Plenty of exercise keeps people healthy. Swimming is a sport that exercises the muscles all over your body.

There are different ways of playing sport. Some sports, such as archery, are played by one person.

Other sports, such as tennis, are played in pairs or foursomes.

Team sports, such as football, teach people to work together towards winning a goal.

Playing for fun and money

Someone who plays sport only for fun is called an amateur. People who are paid to compete, and who earn their living from sport, are called professionals.

What is the most popular sport?

Football is played all over the world. It began in England in the Middle Ages when people from different villages played in the streets and is now enjoyed by millions of people.

The hero's race

A marathon is a 49.195km running race. The first marathon was run by a Greek soldier in 490BC. He ran to deliver news of a victory over the Persians, but then later died of exhaustion.

The first Olympic Games

Discus   Javelin

The Ancient Greeks held games every four years. Women were not allowed to take part or watch them. Sports, such as throwing the javelin, date back to these games.

The modern Olympic Games

The Olympic Games are held every four years in a different country. Amateur athletes from all around the world compete in them.

The Olympic torch is carried by runners from Athens, in Greece, to the opening ceremony. It is kept burning until the games are over.

Nowadays, both women and men athletes take part in over twenty different sports and events. They are watched by millions on television.

Each winner receives a gold medal, those who come second have silver medals and people who come third are given bronze medals.

The oldest sports

Norwegian rock paintings show that people skied on snow as long ago as the Stone Age.

Over 5,000 years ago, men trained for battle with fighting sports, such as wrestling.

Animal sports

In some sports, such as show jumping, people and animals compete together.

Some people shoot animals and birds for fun. These are called 'blood sports'.

New sports

New inventions have led to new sports, such as flying, hang-gliding and motor racing.

The first motor race was held on a course between Paris and Rouen in France in 1894.

Writing and books

People write to keep a record of things that have happened. In the past, people kept records in other ways.

Some North American Indians wove shells into belts and circles. The patterns were a record of tribal meetings.

In Peru, people used to tie knots in strings to keep a record. A bunch of strings was called a 'quipu'.

Who were the first people to write?

The Egyptians and Sumerians invented picture writing about 5,000 years ago. The Egyptian picture writing is called hieroglyphics*.

The Sumerians pressed with a reed pen onto a clay tablet. Later on, their picture writing changed into wedge shaped designs.

Learning the alphabet

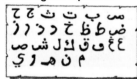

Most of the alphabets people use today probably came from earlier picture writing.

The Roman letter 'A' may have come from an older picture sign for an ox.

People write in different directions. Chinese can be written downwards or across.

From papyrus to paper

The Egyptians wrote on paper made of flattened papyrus. They made ink from charcoal, mixed with water and glue.

Later on, people made parchment from animal skins. It was better than papyrus as they could write on both sides.

The Chinese invented paper made from the bark of mulberry trees. Arab traders brought the secret to Europe.

*You can read more about hieroglyphics on page 67.

The first books

It was not until the Middle Ages that books began to look like they do today, with covers, pages and pictures.

In monasteries, monks called scribes learnt to write. They copied books and decorated them with beautiful drawings.

It took a long time to make each book by hand and only rich people and churches could afford them.

Printing machines

The first printing machine was invented about 550 years ago by a German, called Johann Gutenberg. It was worked by hand.

Modern printing presses make coloured pictures by printing one colour after another. Each sheet of paper contains several pages of the book.

Reading with your fingers

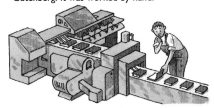

The printed pages are folded so they are in the right order. They are then cut to size and bound together to make a book.

Books for blind people are printed with raised dots, called the Braille alphabet. Patterns of dots stand for different letters and blind people can 'read' the letters with their fingertips.

Art

People often disagree about art. One person may think a painting or sculpture is beautiful but another person may think it is very ugly.

A work of art can be made in many different ways. Each of these artists is working on a different type of art, using different materials.

Sculpture

Painting

Mosaics

Drawing

Architecture

Clay modelling

Wood carving

In the mind's eye

Artists may work from real life and copy what they see.

Some artists may only use what they see in their mind.

Many artists mix real life and their imagination to create a work of art.

Art changes with the times

Different styles of art go in and out of fashion as people's tastes change. Until about 500 years ago, most of the pictures painted by European artists were of religious scenes.

Some art, such as Chinese painting, is traditional. This means that artists have all worked in the same way for hundreds of years without changing their style.

People may be so used to certain styles of art that they are shocked or amused when an artist tries something new.

New types of art are often the result of new inventions. When the camera was invented people took up photography as an art form.

Fame, fortune and forgery

Some artists worked all their lives but no one bought their paintings and they were very poor. They only became famous after they had died.

In the past, wealthy people called patrons paid an artist to work for them because they believed the artist had talent.

Works of art by famous people and ancient works of art are often very valuable. They sell at auctions for very high prices.

Clever forgers can imitate famous artists' work so well that people are fooled. They pay a lot of money for something that is a fake.

Music

What is music?

Music is lots of sounds put together to make a tune.

Not everyone likes the same sort of music.

The oldest music

People probably first made music by singing or chanting long ago.

Why play music?

Music helps people work. Galley slaves on ships used to row in time to drum beats.

How sounds are made

There are three main types of instrument which are played in different ways.

Instruments which you play by blowing are called wind instruments.

Instruments which you play by tapping or banging are called percussion instruments.

Stringed instruments have strings which you pluck or stroke with a bow.

A person who sings alone is called a soloist. Two people singing together is a duet.

A choir is a group of people who sing together or sing different parts of the same song.

People play music to celebrate special occasions such as birthdays and weddings.

Usually people play music to entertain themselves and their friends.

Passing music on

Traditional music, called folk music, is often so old that no one can remember who first wrote it. Some folk music, such as Scottish reels, have become popular around the world.

In the Middle Ages, people invented a way of writing down music. People who write music are called composers. They may write music for one instrument, for many instruments, or songs.

The orchestra

An orchestra is a large group of musicians who play music on many different instruments.

The musicians watch a conductor, who signals them to join in and keeps them playing together.

Bands

Brass band

Jazz band

Steel band

Bands are small groups of players who may play only one sort of music on their instruments.

Some bands have instruments which they can play as they walk around. Others stay in one place.

Crafts

What are crafts?

All through the ages people have hand made things to use in their everyday lives. They often decorate what they have made so that they look colourful and attractive.

People around the world are skilled at different crafts. All these craftspeople are at work on their speciality.

English basket making

Mexican weaving

Turkish carpet making

Pueblo pottery from New Mexico

Spanish lace making

Greek wool spinning

African gold jewellery

Moroccan cloth dyeing

Venetian glass blowing

Mastering a craft

In the Middle Ages, boys called apprentices worked in their master's workshop for seven years, learning a craft.

Craftsmen were proud of their work and employed 'searchers' to stop shoddy work from leaving the workshop.

A master craftsman was someone who had finished his apprenticeship and was an expert in his trade.

Crafts for sale

For thousands of years people have taken their craftwork to open air markets to sell.

Sometimes they exchange their work for things they need but do not know how to make.

In the past, travelling traders and merchants went from country to country.

They bought wares from craftsmen in one place and then sold them somewhere else.

Endangered crafts

Things made by hand are never exactly the same. Many craftworkers sign their work.

In the past, craftworkers often knew their customers and could make things to suit them.

Later on, people invented machines which could make lots of identical things.

The machines were much faster and cheaper than craftspeople so many old crafts died out.

Making up for lost time

Fine examples of some crafts are now valuable.

This is because a lot of craftwork was made for everyday use, and so was thrown away if it broke.

Some people are interested in learning old crafts so that they become popular again and do not die out.

They often sell their work as souvenirs to tourists.

Dressing up

Why do people wear clothes?

People usually wear clothes that suit the work they do, or their way of life.

In some jobs people wear uniforms to be recognized.

Important people wear clothes that show their power, authority and position.

Sports clothes are light and easy for players to wear and move around in.

Some people like to wear clothes that attract attention and make them stand out.

People who want to show they belong to a special group often wear the same sort of clothes.

Keeping up with fashion

The way people dress changes with the times they live in. Four hundred years ago men wore high heels and stockings.

Clothes that were once very popular often seem ridiculous to people who live now.

Clothes that were once thought very daring and shocking are now considered quite ordinary.

Clothes for climates

People who live in hot, damp places wear very little and so keep cool.

In hot, dry climates people wear loose robes to shield them from the Sun.

In cold climates people wear many layers of clothing. Air trapped between the layers helps to keep out the cold.

Old and new clothes

A country's traditional dress, such as the Indian sari, is called their national costume.

Most modern clothes are made by machines. They are easy to wash, cheap and comfortable.

Some people pay a fortune to have clothes specially made for them by a famous fashion designer.

Other ways of dressing up

Masai men, who live in East Africa, spend days doing each other's hair.

The women shave their heads as a sign of beauty, and wear many necklaces.

Long ago in Europe, it was the fashion to hide your hair under an elaborate wig.

People have worn make-up and painted and decorated their bodies since prehistoric times.

Some people, such as the Nuban men from Sudan, paint their bodies all over to make them look strong and healthy.

Tattoos are made by pricking the skin in a pattern and then rubbing in dyes from rocks or plants.

People dress up with jewellery. In Laos, women wear the family savings to show their wealth.

Some people wear jewellery to show they are married. Indian women wear nose rings.

Sometimes the jewellery a person wears shows that they belong to one religion. Christians may wear a cross.

Myths

Long ago people made up stories to explain mysteries and things that they did not understand, such as thunder and lightning. These stories are called myths.

Many of the Ancient Greek myths were about their gods. They thought the gods often appeared on Earth as real people. Zeus, king of the gods, made thunder to frighten his enemies.

How did the world begin?
A North American myth

In this myth, a raven created the world. He dropped pebbles into the ocean to make land. Then he created the trees and grass, fish, birds and animals. Finally he made men and women out of pieces of clay and wood.

A Nigerian myth

In this myth, Mother Woyengi sat on a special stone and made people out of handfuls of earth.

She put the people who chose lives of luxury into a fast, dangerous stream, the others into a slow, clear stream.

A Norse myth
In this old Norse myth, the middle of the universe was a huge tree called Ash Ygdrasil.

For nine nights, Odin, the one-eyed god, hung upside down from the tree to learn poetry, the secret of magic.

King Arthur and the knights of the round table

The Celtic myths about King Arthur told throughout medieval Europe and ever since, are based on a real king who once ruled in Britain.

Arthur had 1,600 good and brave knights. In the stories, they fought many battles against invading enemies, rescued people and killed monsters.

Can myths change history?

The Aztecs of South America told stories about Quetzalcoatl, a fair-skinned god, who would come to Earth.

When the Spanish explorer, Cortes, sailed to South America, the Aztecs thought he was their god.

They brought him gold and gifts and Cortes easily conquered them and took their land.

Dragons

Stories about dragons have been told all over the world for centuries. Hawaii, China, Wales and Iceland all have places named after them.

Dragons usually lived in water and frightened people by breathing fire. Heroes in myths often have to kill a dragon to save everyone's life.

Heroes

Creatures great and small

Many myths tell the adventures of a hero who is searching for something special, such as the secret of life.

In an Ancient Greek myth, a giant called Atlas held the world on his shoulders to stop it falling from the sky.

Tiny spirit people are called fairies. Leprechauns are Irish fairies who must give gold to anyone who can catch them.

Modern myths

Myths can be about the future as well as the past. Today, many films are about heroes travelling through time and space to new worlds.

Stories about the future are called science fiction. Like ancient myths they are based on people's latest theories about the universe.

Religions

People who follow a particular religion believe in a spiritual world and share the same ideas about life and death.

There are many religions around the world. Each one has its own beliefs, customs and rules for how its followers should behave.

Judaism

Jewish people believe that a man called Abraham first told people to believe in God.

They believe that God chose them to keep his laws, which are written in the first part of the Bible.

Christianity

Christians believe God sent his son, Jesus, to teach people how to live. His story is told in the second part of the Bible.

Christians say Jesus taught them to love one another, to pray and teach other people about God. They worship in a church.

Islam

A prophet called Muhammad, from Mecca, taught his followers, Muslims, to pray five times a day to their god, Allah.

Their religion is called 'Islam'. Muslims should obey Allah by praying, fasting (not eating for a while) and helping the poor.

Hinduism

Hindus believe that after you die, you are born again, either as an animal or as another person. If you have been good during your first life, your next life will be a better one. At Hindu festivals, dancers dress up as gods, such as Ganesh, the elephant-god. Most Hindus believe their gods are really all one god, called Brahma, in disguise.

Buddhism

A man named Gautama (later called Buddha) began Buddhism among Hindus in India. Buddhism spread throughout Asia. In Bangkok, Thailand, there is a line of 394 golden statues of Buddha.

Buddhists believe you should give up your luxuries and live a simple, peaceful life. They say that you live more than once, but eventually you can escape to a place of spiritual peace.

Religions without gods

Some eastern religions, like Taoism, have no gods. Taoists say everything in life is sacred because it is part of nature.

They believe all things are either female (called Yin) or male (called Yang). Yin and Yang balance each other.

Taoists want people to live simply and to fit in with nature. They should try to be like a stick floating in a stream.

Rituals

Nearly every small community or tribe in the world has a religion, with its own rituals, songs and dances.

What do witch doctors do?

Some peoples, such as American Indians, believe that sickness and bad luck are caused by evil spirits.

They ask their witch doctors to drive the evil spirits from their homes, using beads, feathers and pipes.

Where do dead people go?

Some people believe that you go to another world as an invisible spirit when you die.

People put flowers on graves to show they have not forgotten the person who has died.

Ancient Egyptians made offerings of food and drink to their dead relatives in the Next World.

Theatre and dance

Why do people dance?

Dancing probably began as a way for people to celebrate something or to worship gods.

People also danced to tell a story, to make their crops grow or to bring luck in a fight.

Formal dancing began at court for women to show off their beautiful dresses.

Nowadays, people dance to keep fit, meet others, follow the latest fashion and for fun.

New dances, such as the tango and the twist, were laughed at until they became popular.

Inventing dances

Choreographers are people who make up the movements and steps dancers perform.

Ways of dancing

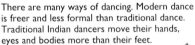

There are many ways of dancing. Modern dance is freer and less formal than traditional dance. Traditional Indian dancers move their hands, eyes and bodies more than their feet.

Russian dancers crouch down and kick out their feet very fast, whirling dervishes stomp and twirl in rhythm and Spanish flamenco dancers stamp in time to the music.

What is ballet?

A simple form of ballet began two hundred years ago at the Italian and French royal courts.

Classical ballet is a difficult dance done on the toes which takes years of training to learn.

The Russians made ballet more exciting by making the music and dance tell a story.

Where did theatre begin?

People have always acted out stories, but the Ancient Greeks built the first theatres. People could go and watch plays.

Actors wore frowning masks if they were in a tragedy (a sad play), and smiling masks if they were in a comedy (a happy one).

Travelling players

In the Dark Ages there were no theatres in Europe. Acrobats, minstrels and jugglers travelled around entertaining people.

Behind the scenes at the theatre

Powerful lights shine on the main actors as they speak. Someone controls the lights from the side of the stage.

Actors often dress up in costumes to look like the person they are supposed to be in a play.

Wings

Curtains

A director tells the actors how to act their part in the play, when to move and how to say their speeches.

Footlights

Scenery and props (objects used in the play) are often put on the stage to make it look more realistic.

The person who writes the play is called a dramatist.

Opera

In an opera, the actors sing their lines to music instead of speaking them. Operas usually have an orchestra, fine costumes and scenery. They were first performed in Italy.

What is mime?

Mime means acting without words. The mime artist shows his feelings by making faces and moving his body. In Japan whole plays, called Kabuki, are acted in mime.

Education

What is education?

Some teachers think that children are like pots, waiting to be filled with information.

Others think teaching should be like lighting a fire – one question leads to many ideas.

Education can mean finding out how to do things and learning how they were done before.

Why learn things?

People learn things for many different reasons.

You can write things down if you want to remember them or share them with others.

Learning a foreign language helps you to understand someone from another country.

Most people around the world learn the things they need to survive, such as how to grow food and build their homes.

Finding out about numbers and how things work helps people to cope with machines and money.

Nowadays many people have more free time to learn sports and hobbies and other ways of having fun together.

When do you learn?

The minute you are born, you start learning by copying people around you. You learn a lot before you are five.

When you go to school, you are taught basic things you need to know. Trying something out is a good way of learning.

No matter how old you are, you can learn something new. Someone who knows all about a subject is called a specialist.

Education in other times and places

In Sparta, in Ancient Greece, boys were trained to be fit and brave so that they could fight their enemies.

In the past, girls were taught different things from boys, such as sewing and cooking. This is still true in some places today.

Two hundred years ago there were few schools. Children of rich families were taught at home by a tutor.

The first free schools were set up in the Industrial Revolution, when many people began to live and work in big cities.

Not everyone has a choice about what to learn. Mexicans in Patzcuaro have to learn how to make hats for a living.

These Bolivian children are having fun at school learning a traditional dance. One day their own children may learn it.

Education today

Only about half the world's children go to school and many go only for a few years.

As well as ordinary schools, there are schools that teach special skills.

People of all ages can go to these schools to learn all kinds of different subjects.

When they leave school, some people go to a college to learn more about a subject.

Inventions such as television and computers have made new ways of learning possible.

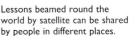

Lessons beamed round the world by satellite can be shared by people in different places.

Government and politics

What is a government?

If people lived together without any rules, they would probably disagree about decisions and get in a muddle.

To avoid this, they choose a few people to organize things and make laws. This is called the government.

What is politics?

Politics is about people deciding how to live together. The ones who think the same way form political parties.

Leaders

A dictator is a leader who decides how to run the country without asking the people what they want. He does not let his people vote. Some kings and emperors were dictators.

If a leader refuses to listen to what people want, they sometimes get angry and take over the government of the country by force. This is called a revolution.

Why do people vote?

In most countries, people choose who they want to run the country for them in an election held every few years.

The country is split up into areas and you vote for someone from your area. Those who win the most votes form the government.

People who want to be in the government try to win votes by promising to run the country in a better way.

Can you change things?

People who get together to try to change something are called a pressure group. They pressurize the government to make new laws. If there are enough of them, this often works.

Until 1918 women in Britain were not allowed to vote. Many joined a pressure group called the suffragettes. They held demonstrations and tied themselves to railings to get what they wanted.

What governments do

The government looks after many different parts of everyday life.

People pay money called 'taxes' to provide all these things:

The government is responsible for the country's roads, and may also run the airlines and railways.

The government looks after education in schools and colleges. It pays for research in art and science.

The government provides a police force, courts and judges to keep law and order.

Some governments take care of people's health by paying for hospitals and doctors.

When countries trade with each other the government helps things to run smoothly.

Most countries keep armed forces and weapons in case there is a war.

Some governments build parks, museums, and places for people to enjoy themselves.

Air and water

What is air?

The Earth is wrapped in a layer of air, called the atmosphere. Air is made of several different gases, one of which is oxygen which people and animals need to breathe to stay alive.

Air is all around you, but you cannot see it. You can feel it, but only when the wind is blowing against you. The wind is moving air.

Air spreads

Air does not have any special shape. It spreads out in all directions and is everywhere.

Air pushes

If you continually blow air into a balloon, it will eventually burst as the air pushes inside the balloon.

A falling parachute traps air underneath it. The air pushes up against the parachute, making it fall slowly.

Hot air rises

When air is heated, it expands and takes up more space. It is lighter than the cold air around it and rises upwards.

Hot air balloons lift off the ground because hot air inside them makes them lighter than the air around them.

A gas burner heats the air inside the balloon. When it is switched off, the air inside it cools and the balloon lands.

Trapped air

Trapped air stops heat escaping. Wool clothes keep you warm because woollen fibres trap lots of air.

Birds fluff up their feathers in winter to trap air under their feathers to keep them warm.

Air presses

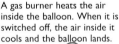

Air presses against you, but your body is made so that you do not feel the weight.

What is water?

Water is liquid. It has no shape of its own, but takes the shape of whatever is holding it.

If water is poured into a glass it will fill the glass, and become the same shape as the inside of the glass.

If water is spilt on the floor, it runs all over the place, because it has nothing to keep it in a particular shape.

Where does water go?

A puddle of water will dry up on a sunny day. The water does not really disappear. It turns into tiny drops, too small for you to see.

The drops, called water vapour, rise into the air. When water turns into vapour and rises into the air, it is called evaporation.

The air is full of water vapour, because heat from the Sun makes water evaporate from the sea, lakes and rivers.

As water vapour rises it reaches cold air high in the sky. It turns back into tiny drops of water which join to make clouds.

As the drops get larger they fall to the ground as rain. Water vapour turning into water again is called condensation.

Water pushes

If you stand in a swimming pool with water up to your neck and your arms by your sides, your arms will slowly rise. The water pushes them up.

Why does an iron ship float?

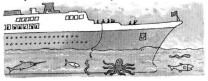

An iron ship floats because it contains air, which is lighter than water. As the ship pushes aside water, the water pushes back, holding the ship afloat.

Light and colour

Nearly all our light comes from the Sun. Light from the Sun gives us days and nights. As the Earth spins around the Sun, the side facing the Sun has daylight, while the other side is dark.

Light travels in straight lines. It cannot go around things. So there are dark shadows behind things that stand in its way.

Things that light can pass through, like glass, are called transparent. Things it cannot pass through, like people, are called opaque.

Splitting light

In 1666, Isaac Newton let a beam of sunlight shine through a piece of glass called a prism.

The light that came out of the prism was broken up into all the colours of the rainbow.

Newton had discovered that white light is made up of many colours mixed together.

What makes a rainbow?

When sunlight shines through rain, we sometimes see a rainbow, because each drop of water behaves like a tiny prism.

The raindrops break light into its different colours, making a rainbow. Rainbow colours are always in the same order.*

From the ground, a rainbow looks like an arch. From an aeroplane it looks like a circle.

*You may not always see all the colours in a rainbow.

Bouncing light

Light bounces off surfaces just like a ball bounces off things. This is called reflection.

If you shine a torch on a mirror, you can see light bounce. All light you see is reflected.

The sunlight that enters our atmosphere is reflected by millions of tiny bits of dust and droplets of water.

In a cinema you see the beam of light between the projector and screen because dust in the air reflects the light.

Black Space

Outer Space is totally dark because there is no dust or water to reflect light.

The Moon has no light of its own. You can only see it because it reflects the light from the Sun.

Why do we see colours?

We see colours because things absorb or reflect light of different colours.

When light shines on snow, all the light is reflected back, so the snow looks white.

When light shines on soot, all the light is absorbed, so the soot looks black.

A red flower looks red because it reflects the red part of light, and absorbs the rest.

A green car reflects the green part of light and absorbs the rest, so it looks green.

Seeing red?

Most animals cannot see colour. A bull charges at a red flag because it is waved, not because it is red.

Electricity

Electricity that stays

If it is dark you may also see a spark.

There are two sorts of electricity. One is called static electricity. It stays in the same place. You can sometimes hear it crackle when you take off nylon clothes.

Electricity that moves

The other sort of electricity is called current electricity. It flows through things. This sort of electricity is used to light and heat our houses, and is used to run machinery.

Discovering electricity

The Greeks knew 2,500 years ago, that rubbing amber with fur made sparks of static electricity. Scientists did not learn how to make current electricity until about 150 years ago.

Electric machines

Michael Faraday invented the first electric motor in 1821. Machines run by electric motors are now used in many houses and in factories, where they do the work of many people.

Conductors

Some substances, like metals, allow electricity to flow through them. They are called conductors. Metal wires are used to conduct electricity from one place to another.

Insulators

Substances electricity cannot flow through, like plastic and rubber, are called insulators. Wires that carry electricity are covered in plastic to protect people from electric shocks.

How does a battery work?

A battery makes electricity with special chemicals. When all the chemicals are used up, the battery stops working.

Electricity from batteries is not as powerful as electricity from plugs. But batteries can be taken and used anywhere.

Danger!

ELECTRICITY CAN GIVE YOU A DANGEROUS ELECTRIC SHOCK. NEVER PLAY WITH PLUGS OR WALL SOCKETS OR ANYTHING THAT IS PLUGGED IN.

Where does electricity come from?

The electricity in our houses, streets and factories is made in big power stations by machines called generators.

The power stations make electricity with fast running water from rivers, or by using the heat from burning coal or oil, or from nuclear power.

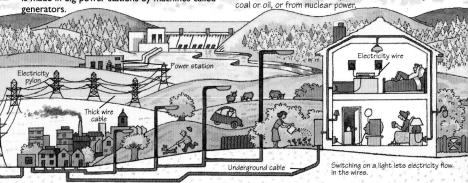

Electricity wire

Power station

Electricity pylon

Thick wire cable

Underground cable

Switching on a light lets electricity flow in the wires.

Electricity flows from power stations along thick wire cables. The cables are carried high above the ground by pylons to towns.

In towns, the cables run underground to each house. The electricity is then carried around the house through wires built into the walls.

What's in a plug?

Plugs have metal prongs which allow electricity to flow through them. When a plug is put into a socket and switched on, electricity flows through the prongs and along the wires.

Why does a light bulb make light?

Electricity flows through a coil of special metal in a light bulb. The metal becomes so hot that it glows white, giving out light. The first light bulb was made in 1879 by Thomas Edison.

Lightning is electric

During thunderstorms, static electricity may jump between a cloud and the ground. It makes a powerful flash of light, called lightning, and can damage or set fire to anything it strikes.

Lightning always takes the shortest route to the ground, so it is dangerous to shelter under a tree during a storm. Tall buildings have metal conductors to carry lightning safely to earth.

Sound

What is sound?

Sound happens when air vibrates, moving very quickly backwards and forwards. When you speak, cords at the back of your throat, called vocal cords, vibrate, so making the air vibrate.

The vibrations push the air, so that the air vibrates too. These invisible vibrations, called sound waves, spread out through the air, like the ripples when you drop a stone in a pond.

How do you hear?

Sound waves make tiny pieces of skin in your ears, called eardrums, vibrate and send messages to your brain.

The speed of sound

Sound waves travel at about 340 metres per second. When an aircraft flies faster than sound, you hear a bang.

Thunderstorms

In a storm you see lightning before you hear thunder because light travels faster than sound.

Silent space

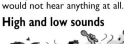

Radio waves can travel through space.

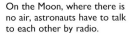

Sound waves need air to travel through. If there was no air you would not hear anything at all.

On the Moon, where there is no air, astronauts have to talk to each other by radio.

Echo! Echo!

Sound waves sometimes bounce off surfaces, such as the underneath of bridges. When this happens you hear an echo.

High and low sounds

The faster something vibrates, the higher the sound it makes. The vibration made by a mosquito beating its wings up and down very fast makes a very high sound.

A bee beats its wings more slowly than a mosquito, making a lower sound. The highness or lowness of sound is called its pitch and the number of vibrations a second is its frequency.

Animal hearing

Many animals can hear sounds that are too high pitched for people to hear.

Dogs can hear sounds from much further away than people. Farmers use special whistles to send them signals from far away.

Telephone

The telephone was invented in 1875 by Alexander Bell. There are now over 500 million telephones in the world.

On the telephone, the vibrations made by your voice are turned into electric signals by a microphone.

Wires carry these signals over long distances, so you can telephone people far away. Wires can run under the sea.

The person you call hears your voice because a loudspeaker in their telephone turns the signals back into sound.

Radio waves

Radio waves are all around you, but you cannot hear them. They travel at the speed of light.

Radio stations turn sound waves from voices or music into radio waves and send them through the air.

Radios turn radio waves back into sound waves you can hear. You can listen to many programmes on the radio.

Ships use radios to contact each other or the shore. Aircraft crews use radios to speak to the control tower.

Television pictures

Television pictures are filmed by special cameras that turn pictures into radio waves.

A television set picks up radio waves and turns them back into sound and pictures.

Transport by land

Making tracks

Until about 5,000 years ago there were no roads and people could only go as fast as they could run, so they did not go far. The first roads followed animal tracks, like the bush trails people cut through the forests in Africa.

Dragging loads

To build the pyramids, the Ancient Egyptians needed blocks of stone that were too heavy to drag over the ground. They moved the stones by putting them on wooden sleds and pulling them along on rollers made of tree trunks.

Riding

About 4,000 years ago, people began to tame horses. They could travel ten times faster on horseback than on foot.

Harnessing

At about the same time the harness was invented. Now people could use strong animals to pull heavy loads.

On the road

About 2,000 years ago the Romans built thousands of kilometres of straight roads paved with slabs of rock.

The wheel revolution

The first wheels were probably made about 5,000 years ago by the Sumerian people. They built carts and fixed solid wooden wheels to them, to carry food to trade with other villages.

The Ancient Greeks used chariots on wheels to go to war. They put spokes in the wheels to make the chariots lighter and faster and added wooden rims so that the wheels lasted longer.

Carriages and coaches

About 250 years ago rich people in Europe rode in horse-drawn carriages. Roads were bumpy, so travel was uncomfortable.

Stage coaches were the first kind of public transport. Every 20km or so they stopped at an inn to change the team of horses.

Crossing America in a wagon

The pioneers of the nineteenth century travelled vast distances across North America and South Africa in covered wagons.

A team of oxen or horses pulled them. Inside there was room for a family and enough food and water to last for weeks of travel.

The age of the train

In 1825, the first steam train to carry passengers ran from Darlington to Stockton, in Britain, at 24 km/h.

People could travel further and faster by train. By the 1930s a train called *Hiawatha* was able to cross the USA at 160 km/h.

Most trains run on diesel fuel or electricity. In Japan the world's busiest railway carries more than 112,000 people daily.

How the car started

Two German engineers, Benz and Daimler, built the first petrol-driven car in the 1880s.

Early cars had wooden, spoked wheels, oil lamps, and no roof. They often broke down.

In 1889, John Dunlop invented air-filled rubber tyres to give a smoother ride.

At first, cars were built by hand and were very expensive. Between 1908 and 1928, Henry Ford produced 20 million cheaper cars in a factory in the USA, so many more people could buy them.

Cars with powerful engines and bodies shaped to cut through the wind can travel very fast. In 1997, a car called *Thrust SSC*, with a jet engine, went at over 1,200 km/h in Nevada, USA.

Ships

Setting sail

The Egyptians built the first ships out of reeds 5,000 years ago, to cross the River Nile.

They had a papyrus reed sail which helped them move when the wind was behind them.

When they wanted to sail into the wind, the sailors had to row the ship along.

Round ships

For thousands of years, Arab traders have built small ships, called dhows, to carry cargo. They have triangular sails which can be turned to catch the wind and sail in any direction.

Long ships

The Vikings of Scandinavia were the first to cross the Atlantic to North America in about AD900. Their sturdy ships had a big square sail and were steered by a large oar.

Voyages of discovery

By 1500, ships in Northern Europe had grown very big, with up to four masts and many sails. In these ships, explorers discovered routes across the Atlantic and to India and China.

Sailors climbed the masts to let out or take in the sails.

The ships were steered with a rudder.

A sailor's life was hard and dangerous. Sailors slept in a dark, crowded room under the deck, and lived on salted meat, dry biscuits and water.

Clippers

In the 1880s, huge, sleek cargo ships, called clippers, raced to carry tea from China to Britain and wool from Australia to the USA.

With their tall masts and many sails, they could travel up to 640km in 24 hours, in a strong wind, and could cross the Atlantic in 14 days.

Steam ships

In 1838, the first wooden ships to be driven by steam engines crossed the Atlantic.

Steam turned paddle wheels on each side and they had sails in case they ran out of coal.

Propellers

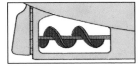

In the 1850s, iron ships were driven by a screw propeller. They could follow timetables, as they no longer relied on wind.

Luxury liners

During the 1930s huge steel ships called liners were built to carry passengers between Europe and North America in great comfort and luxury.

Oil tankers

One of the largest ships ever built is the oil tanker, *Globtik London*. It is 379m long, so the crew use bicycles to get around on deck.

Nuclear submarines

In 1960, a US nuclear-powered submarine went around the world, underwater, in only 83 days at depths of 300 metres.

Hovercraft

A hovercraft can travel over flat land or water. It skims along on a cushion of air made by powerful fans.

Hydrofoils

Hydrofoils are the fastest type of watercraft. They have underwater wings to lift and speed them above the water.

Flying machines

Taking off

For hundreds of years people tried to fly by copying birds. They built wings from feathers and jumped from high places.

They always crashed because human chest muscles cannot flap wings fast enough to keep a human body in the air.

Balloons

Since 1783 people have flown in baskets lifted by balloons filled with hot air, but they only go the way the wind blows.

Gliding down

In 1891, a German named Otto Lilienthal ran down a hill strapped to a hang-glider he had built. The air trapped under the wings lifted him off the ground and he glided gently down.

The Wright flyer

The Wright brothers made the first powered aeroplane flight of 36.5 metres in 1903. They built their own petrol engine to drive two propellers fixed to a glider frame.

Record breakers

Early aeroplanes were light and unstable, and the engines often failed. Flying them was exciting but dangerous.

In 1909, Louis Blériot made the first powered flight across the Channel from France to England in only 37 minutes.

Amy Johnson flew from England to Australia in 1930. It took 19 days because she had to stop to refuel her plane.

Passenger flights

By the 1930s, aircraft with four engines were able to carry up to 30 passengers as fast as 193 km/h. Flying became a fast and comfortable way to travel a long distance.

Modern jumbo jet aircraft can carry hundreds of passengers at speeds of up to 969 km/h. Flying has become so popular that every minute an aircraft lands somewhere in the world.

Supersonic speed

Aircraft that go faster than the speed of sound are called supersonic. When they reach that speed they make a loud bang.

The first supersonic jet to carry passengers is Concorde. It travels at 2,333 km/h, and can fly from New York to London in three hours.

Helicopters

A helicopter has a propeller on its roof to lift it straight upwards, so it can take off from any piece of ground.

Helicopters cannot fly faster than 300 km/h, but they fly up and down as well as along, and they can hover in one place.

They are useful for dropping cargo or rescuing people from the sea or on mountains where aircraft cannot land.

Rocketing into space

Rockets travel faster than any other craft. They shoot into the air pushed by hot gases made by burning liquid fuel.

By the 1960s, the Americans and Soviets had built huge rockets powerful enough to carry people into Outer Space.

In 1969, a rocket called *Apollo 11* flew 384,400km to the Moon in three days, and a man landed there for the first time.

Space shuttles

Space shuttles use rockets to take off, but they have wings and land like aircraft.

Rockets can only be used once, but space shuttles can carry scientists on many trips to Outer Space.

Medicine

What is medicine?

Medicine is not just what you take when you are ill. It also means how to cure people and stop them from getting ill.

What is illness?

A lot of illness is caused by germs getting into the body. Germs are tiny living things, so small that you cannot see them.

Your body reacts to these germs, producing visible signs such as a rash, or invisible signs (called symptoms) such as a headache.

Seeing the doctor

When you are ill, the doctor finds out what is wrong by studying the signs and symptoms. Each illness has its own signs and symptoms.

The doctor may say you need medicine. There are thousands of medicines and the doctor has to choose the right one for you.

Danger!

ALL MEDICINES CAN BE DANGEROUS.

NEVER PLAY WITH THEM AND NEVER TAKE ANY MEDICINE WITHOUT ASKING A GROWN-UP FIRST.

Medicines

Antibiotics are medicines that work by killing the germs in your blood which make you ill. The first one, penicillin, was discovered in 1928.

Some medicines, called analgesics, can make you feel better. They lower your temperature and make the pain go away, but they do not kill the germs. Aspirin is an analgesic.

Other cures

Some people have other ways of curing illness. Acupuncturists push fine needles into the skin, without hurting the patient.

Homeopathic doctors use tiny amounts of medicines made from plants and minerals to treat illnesses.

First Aid

First Aid is the first thing you do to help someone if they have an accident. Knowing what to do may save their life.

Preventing illnesses

Preventing people from becoming ill is as important as curing illness. Looking after your body by eating healthy food and taking exercise makes you healthier and can prevent illness.

Vaccines

A vaccine is a small dose of germs that makes your body produce the substances to fight those germs. This stops you getting the disease in the future.

Hospitals

People go to hospital for tests and special treatments. Sometimes they need an operation. Most mothers also have their babies in hospital.

Medical scientists study samples, such as blood, taken from patients.

Nurses do a lot of different jobs looking after patients. Midwives help mothers to have their babies.

Specially trained doctors called surgeons do operations in a room called the operating theatre.

Everyone wears specially cleaned clothes, rubber gloves and masks to stop germs spreading.

Patients are given an injection to make them sleep deeply so that they do not feel any pain.

X-ray pictures of your insides are taken to see if any bones are broken.

Specialists are experts on one part of the body, such as the bones.

Blood Bank

Blood is stored in a Blood Bank. It is given to anyone who has lost a lot of their blood in an accident.

What makes things go?

Things do not move by themselves. Something must push or pull them.

The Earth pulls

You have to push a ball into the air by throwing or kicking it. The ball comes back to the ground because of gravity.

Gravity is the pull of the Earth which attracts everything to it. You cannot see gravity but you can see what it does.

Gravity makes leaves fall to the ground and rivers run downhill. If there was no gravity, things would spin off the Earth.

Muscle power

Thousands of years ago, people only had their own muscles to do all their own work.

Then they learned to use animals, such as oxen and donkeys to pull ploughs and to carry heavy loads.

They learned to make simple machines, such as levers and pulleys. These made their work easier and faster.

They could use them to lift and build things which were much too heavy to be moved by muscle alone.

Power from nature

People learned to use moving water and wind to work machines.

The Egyptians used wind to push their boats along 5,000 years ago.

The first water-wheels were built about 2,000 years ago along rivers where the current of water turned them.

17th century water-wheel, Syria

They were used to bring water to the fields and to turn millstones that ground grain.

For more than a thousand years, until steam engines came into use, water-wheels were the main source of power for making many machines work.

Greek windmill

Dutch windmill

Windmills depend on wind so they could be built in high places where there were no rivers or streams. The first windmill in Europe dates back to 1150.

Power from steam

The first engine to be invented was the steam engine, about 200 years ago. Steam engines were powerful and could do greater tasks than any of the earlier machines.

They could run huge machines in factories. Early steam engines burnt coal or wood to make them work.*

The first steam railway engine, or locomotive, was built in 1803. For the next 100 years, most trains were pulled by steam locomotives.

American steam locomotive

British steam locomotive

*You can read more about steam engines on pages 72 and 73.

Carriages were invented that were powered by steam engines. They moved very slowly.

Boats driven by steam engines were built a hundred years ago. They were the first boats that could travel without needing the wind or water currents.

Power from inside

A new type of engine, called the internal combustion engine, was invented in 1860. Instead of burning fuel outside the engine, to make steam pass into the engine, it burns fuel inside the engine. This means it can be smaller than a steam engine.

Petrol engines in cars, diesel engines and jet engines are all internal combustion engines.

The first power-driven and controlled flight was made in 1903 by an aeroplane with a petrol engine.

Today, diesel-electric locomotives run high speed passenger trains.

Most passenger aeroplanes today have jet engines. Jet engines have turbines, which are many-bladed wheels that spin very fast.

Many ships today are driven by turbines.

Turbines can be made to spin by burning fuel or by flowing water. Water turbines in dams make a quarter of the world's electricity. This is called hydro-electric power.

Electricity is carried by cables and wires to homes and factories. There it is used to work many different types of machines.*

Rocket engines

Rocket engines work in the same way as jet engines except that rockets carry their own supply of oxygen. They do this because fuel cannot burn without oxygen and there is none in Space.

Making machines go

The fuel for internal combustion engines must be able to flow into the engine to be burnt. It must be liquid, so coal and wood are of no use.

The internal combustion engine was only workable once fuels, such as gas and oil, were discovered in the last century.

Coal and oil are called fossil fuels because they are made from the fossilized remains of plants and animals that lived hundreds of millions of years ago, before the time of dinosaurs.

Today, so much oil is used that there is a danger that the supply will run out.

So people are looking for new ways of making electricity, such as using heat from the Sun or power from the wind.

Wind turbine
Solar panel

Nuclear power

Nuclear power stations make electricity. The first nuclear power station was built in 1954 in what was the USSR and others have now been built in many countries.

Machines and inventions

Over the last 100 years many machines and gadgets have been invented to make homes more comfortable and easier to keep clean.

Vacuum cleaners

The first vacuum cleaner, invented in 1904, had bellows that sucked up dust.

Vacuum cleaners that worked with electric motors were sold in the USA from 1908.

Washing machines

People began to use simple washing machines in the 1900s. Clothes were put into a wooden tub and tumbled by turning a handle.

By 1920 washing machines were fitted with motors, but the clothes still had to be fed by hand through a mangle to wring the water out.

Modern washing machines can be programmed to soak, wash, spin and dry the clothes on their own.

Irons

In the 1850s ironing was a slow task. Irons were heated by blocks of metal warmed in the fire.

By 1890 electrically heated irons had been invented. The latest irons press clothes, having first dampened them with jets of steam.

Baths and showers

Until the 1850s baths had to be filled and emptied by hand so they were usually small and shallow.

One type of bath, built in 1900, had a shower fixed to it. Someone pumped water out of the bath to spray the bather.

By 1900 some baths had cold water piped to the taps. The water was heated by a gas boiler under the bath.

Today most houses have bathrooms, supplied with hot water piped from a central boiler.

Toilets

Toilets that flushed waste into the sewers when a chain was pulled were invented in 1888.

Today toilets are quieter but still work in much the same way.

Cookers

Until the 1800s, cooking was mainly done on open fires, or on iron ranges that burned coal or wood.

In the 1860s gas cookers were invented that could be turned on and off to give heat instantly.

In the 1930s cookers were fitted with thermostats to hold the oven temperature steady.

At the end of the 1950s a new, much faster way of cooking food by microwaves rather than by heat was invented.

Refrigerators

For hundreds of years people have stored food by packing it in ice. In 1890 home refrigerators were invented to keep food cool and fresh.

Between 1912 and 1915 Clarence Birdseye began to freeze food to keep it fresh for longer. Many households now freeze their own food.

Central heating

The first central heating systems, in Ancient Rome, heated the whole house with warm air from a furnace underground.

In the mid 1800s, coal and wood boilers were used to heat radiators.

Some new houses have hot-air vents built into the walls of every room. The air is heated by gas or electricity.

Air conditioning

Air conditioning was first used in the USA in 1911, to cool homes, by pumping hot air out and cool air in.

Clocks

Grandfather pendulum clocks were first made around 1670 in London. They keep accurate time to within 2 minutes a day.

In 1929 quartz chips were used in clocks to make them accurate to within one second in 3 years.

Pins and zips

Safety pins were first made in the USA in 1849. Before that, people used brooches to pin clothes.

A new, quick way of fastening clothes together – the zip – was invented in 1913 by a Swedish engineer.

Sewing machines

Around 1856 people began to use sewing machines worked by hand or foot treadle to make clothes at home.

Nowadays sewing machines are electronic. They can sew many different stitches at the touch of a button.

Lenses

In 1609 Galileo used spectacle lenses to build an early telescope. He used it to see stars that had not been seen before.

Microscopes were invented in Holland in 1590. They magnified tiny things, such as bacteria, through strong lenses.

Cameras

Cameras were invented in 1839. Early cameras took photographs on coated paper or glass, which was very slow.

In 1889 the first portable Kodak cameras were invented. They used a new kind of flexible roll film which meant they could take photos more quickly and cheaply.

Modern cameras are extremely accurate. They can take photos even in the dark and underwater.

Typewriters

Typewriters were invented in the 1870s. Until this century most people in offices wrote everything by hand.

With the latest electronic typewriters some people can type 90 words in a minute.

Record players

Wind-up clockwork record players called gramophones were invented in the 1880s. At first the records were hard to hear.

Modern electric hi-fi systems produce a much clearer sound and play music in stereo out of two speakers.

At first inventors tried to make records out of wax, tinfoil and even chocolate. Today they are made from plastic.

Radios

The first radios were made in the 1920s. They only made a faint sound so people had to listen to them with headphones.

In the 1950s portable radios became possible because transistors were invented. One small transistor can replace many parts radios need.

Televisions

Television began in the 1930s. Early sets had a tiny screen showing flickering black-and-white pictures.

By the 1960s television was being broadcast in colour. Nowadays people with video recorders can record TV programmes or use video cameras to make their own films.*

New technology

Recently, discoveries in electronics have led to a revolution in technology, which has changed the way we live.

Information

In the past, information was stored on paper in the form of books, newspapers or timetables.

People needed huge filing systems and libraries to store information.

Then, at the beginning of the 20th century, people began to experiment with electronics (ways of controlling electricity).

Scientists invented valves which could control the flow of small currents of electricity.

These valves were used as amplifiers in the first radios.

They were also used to make the first computers in the 1940s.

These huge machines filled a whole room. They could do calculations but not much else.

The silicon chip

In 1958 the silicon chip was invented. A chip is a tiny little slice of silicon only a few millimetres square.

Enlarged silicon chip

It contains hundreds of electric circuits and can control almost any machine, as long as they have been programmed to work together.

Lots of machines you use every day, such as washing machines, televisions, cameras and telephones work automatically as they are controlled by chips.

Computers

The invention of the chip meant that people could make smaller, faster computers that could do more than ever before.

The personal computers of today are as powerful as the computers that filled a whole room 50 years ago.

A computer can look up the electronic equivalent of a library of books in a split second, and display information from any page of any of the books.

The first computers could only do calculations. Now, you can draw, paint, play games, and even make music on a computer.

You can also receive information and send messages to other computers on the Internet. The messages go along the telephone lines.

Computer signals are converted into telephone signals by a modem.

Robots

Robots are automatic machines which are controlled by computers.

They can be programmed to do different jobs, but cannot do anything on their own.

Most robots cannot move but stay in one spot. They are like big arms with tools on the end.

They are mainly used in factories to do work that is repetitive or dangerous. They are very strong and tough.

They are also useful for doing jobs in Space in conditions which would be difficult for people.

The space shuttle can be fitted with a long folding robot arm. It uses this to launch satellites and other machines or to repair them when necessary.

New materials

Plastics have revolutionized life both at home and work.

The first plastic was made in 1869 from plant cellulose. It was hard but it could be shaped when heated.

During the 1930s new types of plastic were made from chemicals found in coal.

In 1935 nylon was made from chemicals. It was a cheap copy of silk and was used to make underwear and stockings.

Polyesters were invented in the 1940s. From the 1950s onwards many plastics were made from petroleum-based chemicals.

Modern plastics you use every day include vinyl, silicone polish, adhesives, cling film and plastic bags.

Space exploration

New technology has made the exploration of Space possible.

Satellites are unmanned spacecraft launched by rockets which orbit the Earth. The first, *Sputnik 1*, was launched in 1957 from the former USSR.

Telstar (USA) satellite

There are about 300 satellites in orbit today. They are used to send telephone calls and television pictures around the world and for weather information.

Astronauts have orbited the Earth, walked in Space and have landed on the Moon.

Viking 1 (USA) on Mars

Unmanned spacecraft have explored distant planets. They sent back information and pictures and landed on Mars and Venus. *Voyager 2* (USA) flew by Saturn in 1980, Uranus in 1986, and Neptune in 1989. Mars is a target for human exploration.

Lasers

Lasers are machines which make light. The first was made in 1960.

Torch light

Laser light

Unlike ordinary light which spreads out and is made of many colours, light from a laser remains in a narrow beam and is all of one colour.*

Laser light is the brightest light known, even brighter than the Sun. When it hits and is absorbed by an object, the light energy turns into heat energy. This heat is so strong, it can be used to cut, drill, and weld strong metals.

Laser beam

Drill

Steel

Surgeons use lasers to operate on patients. As well as making a fine cut, the heat from the laser seals up the wound.

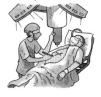

Lasers can make holograms. These are three dimensional photographs: they look like a solid object hanging in the air in front of you. When you look at a hologram from a different angle, you get a different view of the picture.

Information on a compact disc is read by a laser beam and converted into electric signals.

Lasers are used to measure distances by counting how long it takes for the light to reach something.

Earth

Laser beam

Moon

In 1962, a laser was pointed at the Moon to calculate its distance from Earth. Scientists saw the light reflected on the Moon just over two seconds later.

Index

A

abacus, 69
Aborigines, 36
Abraham, 96
acrobats, 25, 66, 99
actors, 99
acupuncturists, 118
AD, dates, 63
adhesives, 125
adventurers, 28
aeroplanes, 7, 74, 110, 111, 116-117, 121
Africa, 6, 25, 28, 30-31, 112, 113
    animals in, 52
    food, 81
    people in, 76, 78, 81, 93
air, 7, 20, 21, 42, 58, 104-105, 116
    heating of, 122
    pollution of, 60
    vibrations of, 110
air conditioning, 122
aircraft, 7, 110, 111, 116, 117
Allah, Muslim god, 96
alligators, 50
alphabet, 84
    Braille, 85
Amazon jungle, 76, 78
Amazon River, 25, 32
American Indians, 84, 97
Americans, 25, 74, 117
Americas, 28, 32-33
amphibians, 40, 41, 51
amplifiers, 124
Amundsen, Roald, explorer, 28
analgesics, 118
Ancient
    Egyptians, 17, 28, 62, 66-67, 84, 112, 114, 120
    Greeks, 28, 62, 82, 94, 95, 99, 101, 108, 112
    Romans, 63, 68-69, 84, 112, 122
    World, 62, 66-69
anemones, 48
Angel Falls, 25
animal hearing, 111
animal sight, 107
animals, 19, 22, 23, 64, 65, 112, 120
    cold-blooded, 50, 51
    evolution of, 40-41
    homes of, 27, 45, 60, 61
    remains of, 15, 121
    sports with, 69, 83
    use of skins, 64, 79, 84
    warm-blooded, 52, 54-55
Antarctica, 6, 23, 37

anteater, 55
antennae, insect, 46
antibiotics, 118
Apollo 11, rocket, 117
apprentice craftsmen, 71, 90
Arab traders, 84, 114
Arabs, Bedouin, 79
archery, 82
architecture, 86
Arctic Circle, 79
Arctic Ocean, 23, 26
arithmetic, 69
armour, 70
Armstrong, Neil, 74
army, Ancient Roman, 63, 69
art, 86-87
arteries, 57
Arthur, King, 94
artists, 86-87
Ash Ygdrasil, 94
Asia, 34-35, 97
asteroids, 9
astronauts, 74, 110, 125
astronomers, 11
Athens, Greece, 83
athletes, 75, 83
Atlantic Ocean, 114, 115
Atlas, Greek giant, 28, 95
atmosphere, 7, 104
atomic clocks, 17
auctions, art, 87
Australia, 27, 36, 51, 74, 116
autumn, 18, 19, 44, 52
axolotl, 51
Aztecs, South American Indians, 28, 95

B

baby animals, 19, 49, 50, 54, 55
baby humans, 55, 76, 119
backbone, 40, 51, 52
Baikal, Lake, 24
ball and socket joints, 56
ballet, 98
balloons, 104
    hot air, 104, 116
ballroom dancing, 98
bands, musical, 89
Bangkok, Thailand, 97
basalt, 14
baths, 69, 122
bats, 54
    long-eared, 45
batteries, 108
battering ram, 69

BC, dates, 63
beaks, bird, 53
bear, polar, 55
beavers, 54
Bedouins, 79
    wedding meal, 81
bees, 47, 110
    hives, 47
    honey, 47
    sting, 46
beetles, 46
beliefs, 96
Bell, Alexander, 111
bellows, 122
Benlomond, boat, 27
Benz, German engineer, 113
Bible, 96
birds, 52-53, 83, 94, 104, 116
Birdseye, Clarence, 122
birds of prey, 53
Black Death, 71
Blériot, Louis, 116
blind, reading when, 85
Blondin, Charles, 25
blood, 46, 56, 57, 58, 119
Blood Bank, 119
'blood sports', 83
boa constrictor, 50
boats, 27, 73, 114-115, 120, 121
body, human, 56-59, 80, 82, 93, 118, 119
boilers, 122
Bolivia, 101
bones, 64, 65, 69
    animal, 54
    bird, 52
    human, 56, 119
    books, 85
Brahma, Hindu god, 96
Braille alphabet, 85
brain, human, 56, 58, 59
Brazil, 32
bread, 80, 81
breathing, 60, 104
    in amphibians, 51
    in animals, 55
    in fish, 49
    in humans, 42, 57, 58, 59
    in plants, 42
bridges, 63, 73
bristlecone pine, 44
Britain, 74, 102, 116
Buddha, 97
Buddhism, 97
bulls, 107
burials, 62, 67, 97
bushmen huts, 78

Conversion tables

Temperature

Converting between °C and °F

$°F = (1.8 \times °C) + 32$
$°C = (°F - 32) \div 1.8$

Water freezes at 0°C (32°F)
Water boils at 100°C (212°F)

Celsius (°C)	Fahrenheit (°F)
-10	14
-5	23
0	32
5	41
10	50
15	59
20	68
25	77
30	86
35	95
40	104
45	113

Weight

1 gram (g)	= 1000 mg (milligrams)
1 kilogram (kg)	= 1000 g
1 tonne (t)	= 1000 kg
1 ounce (oz)	= 28.35 g
1 pound (lb)	= 16 oz

Kilograms (kg)	Pounds (lb)
0.45	1.00
0.5	1.10
1	2.21
2	4.41
3	6.61
4	8.82
5	11.02
6	13.23
7	15.43
8	17.64
9	19.84
10	22.05

Volume

1000 ml (millilitres)	= 1litre (l)
1 UK pint	= 0.57 litres
1 UK gallon	= 4.55 litres
1 US pint	= 0.47 litres
1 US gallon	= 3.79 litres

Litres (l)	UK gallons (gal)
1	0.22
2	0.44
3	0.66
4	0.88
4.5	1.00
5	1.10
6	1.32
7	1.54
8	1.76
9	1.98
10	2.20
100	22.00

Length

1 centimetre (cm)	= 10 millimetres (mm)
1 metre (m)	= 100 cm
1 kilometre (km)	= 1000 m

1 inch (in)	= 2.54 cm
1 foot (ft)	= 12 in
1 yard (yd)	= 3 ft

Centimetres (cm)	Inches (in)
0.1	0.04
1	0.39
2	0.79
2.5	1.00
3	1.18
4	1.57
5	1.97
6	2.36
7	2.76
8	3.15
9	3.54
10	3.94

Metres (m)	Feet (ft)
0.3	1.00
1	3.28
2	6.56
3	9.84
4	13.12
5	16.40
6	19.69
7	22.97
8	26.25
9	29.53
10	32.81
100	328.08

Miles (mi)	Kilometres (km)
0.6	1.00
1	1.61
2	3.22
3	4.83
4	6.44
5	8.05
6	9.66
7	11.27
8	12.88
9	14.48
10	16.09
100	160.93

This edition first published in 2001 by Usborne Publishing Ltd., Usborne House, 83-85 Saffron Hill, London EC1N 8RT, England. www.usborne.com Copyright © 2001, 1998, 1993, 1986 Usborne Publishing Ltd. The name Usborne and the device are Trade Marks of Usborne Publishing Ltd. All rights reserved. No part of this publication may be reproduced, stored in a retrieval system or transmitted in any form or by any means, electronic, mechanical, photocopying, recording or otherwise without the prior permission of the publisher. Printed in Dubai.